ZIMBABWE

A Treasure of Africa

by Al Stark

Dillon Press, Inc.   Minneapolis, Minnesota 55415

Photographs courtesy of the following: Associated Press—65, 69, 147; Ric Bohy—cover, 75, 107; Copley News Service—93; ROTO—63, 130; South African Railways and Harbours Publicity Department, Johannesburg—53 (2); Al Stark/The Detroit News—9, 15, 18-19, 26, 29, 31, 39, 43, 72, 86, 88, 91, 92, 95, 101, 110, 113, 120; United Nations—34, 47, 67 (bottom, UN Photo 164287), 104; United Nations/Camera Press—67 (top right); United Nations/Ciric-Geneva—127, 132; United Nations/Contact—12, 82, 116; United Nations/P. David—58, 74; United Nations/Photo by Y. Nagata—67 (top left); United Press International—137, 144

Library of Congress Cataloging in Publication Data

Stark, Al.
   Zimbabwe, a treasure of Africa.

   (Discovering our heritage)
   Bibliography: p.
   Includes index.
   Summary: Discusses the people, traditions, holidays, religions, schools, history, geography, and wildlife of Zimbabwe, once known as Rhodesia.
   1. Zimbabwe—Juvenile literature. [1. Zimbabwe] I. Title. II. Series.
DT962.S73   1985   968.91   85-6944
ISBN 0-87518-308-5

Dillon Press, Inc., 242 Portland Avenue South
Minneapolis, Minnesota 55415

Printed in the United States of America
  2 3 4 5 6 7 8 9 10 93 92 91 90 89 88 87

Contents

4

Fast Facts About Zimbabwe

Official Name: Republic of Zimbabwe.

Capital: Harare.

Location: Southeast Africa. Countries that border land-locked Zimbabwe include Zambia, Botswana, South Africa, and Mozambique.

Area: 150,800 square miles (390,580 square kilometers); at its widest point it stretches about 540 miles (850 kilometers) east to west, and about 460 miles (750 kilometers) north to south.

Elevation: *Highest*—Mount Inyangani, 8,514 feet (2,595 kilometers) above sea level; *Lowest*—about 2,000 feet (about 620 meters) above sea level, along southern and eastern river basins.

Population: *1985 estimated population*—8,720,000; *Distribution*—76 percent live in rural areas, with 24 percent living in or near cities; *Density*—57 persons per square mile (22 persons per square kilometer).

Form of Government: Republic.

Some Important Products: Coffee, corn, sugar, wheat, tea, cotton, tobacco, cattle; asbestos, chromium, coal, gold; clothing, chemicals, shoes, iron, steel, and other metal products.

Basic Unit of Money: Zimbabwe dollar.

Major Languages: English is the official language. The languages of the two major ethnic groups, the Shona and Ndebele peoples, are also studied in Zimbabwean schools by government order.

Major Religions: Fifty-eight percent Christian, with small numbers of Jewish, Muslim, Hindu, and Bahai practitioners. Many Africans also follow traditional ethnic religions.

Flag: The Zimbabwean flag has seven horizontal stripes: from top to bottom, the colors are green, yellow, red, black, red, yellow, and green. On the left is a white triangle which has in it a Great Zimbabwe bird on a red star.

National Anthem: "Ishe Komborera Africa" ("God Bless Africa").

Major Holidays: Independence Day (April 18); Workers' Day (May 1); Africa Day (May 25); Boxing Day (first weekday after Christmas); Whitsunday (seventh Sunday after Easter).

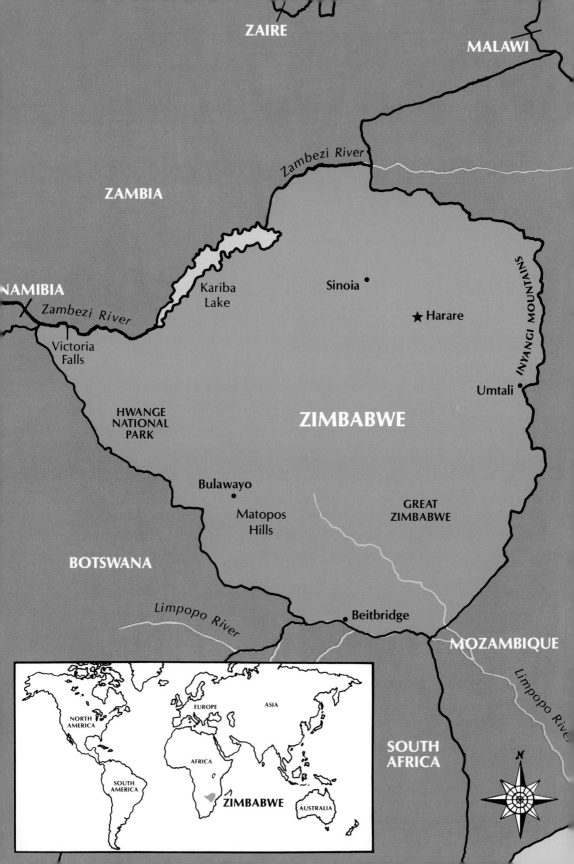

1. Land of Surprises

Say it out loud: Zimbabwe. *(Zim-BOB-wee.)*

Africa, a glorious continent and one of the world's last frontiers, is full of places with names that have music in them. So is Zimbabwe, a nation in southern Africa.

The most important city along Zimbabwe's eastern border is Umtali. Say Umtali out loud. *(Oom-TAH-lee.)*

Hear the music?

Bulawayo is a major manufacturing city in the south of Zimbabwe. In its early days it was a farmer's city, set in the fertile farm-and-ranch belt that runs like a broad green stripe from the top to the bottom of Zimbabwe. The first white settlers drove ox-carts into Bulawayo each Saturday, just the way American farm families used to gather in their own market towns on Saturday mornings.

(Boo-lah-WAY-oh.)

Zimbabwe's northern and southern borders are formed by great rivers, and they, too, have great African names. The river to the north is the Zambezi. Elephants come to drink at the river at dusk when the sky turns orange in the setting sun, a sight for which the Zambezi is famous. The river to the south is the Limpopo.

If you can hear the music when you say Zimbabwe, Umtali, Bulawayo, Zambezi, and Limpopo, it is only fair to give you a warning. The Africa bug is likely to get you.

It is said that most people who get a taste of Africa's adventure and mystery, its wonders and surprises, carry it with them forever. Africa gets under their skin and becomes a part of them. It is that powerful and that fascinating a place.

This isn't true of everyone, of course. Some people take one look at Africa and can't get away quickly enough. But most travelers can't resist its excitement and adventure, and everything they find exciting and adventurous exists in Zimbabwe.

This former British colony for many years was known as Southern Rhodesia or simply Rhodesia. (Its name was changed in 1980.) Zimbabwe is located near the bottom of Africa and slightly to the right of center. Its neighbors are the countries of Zambia, Mozambique, South Africa, and Botswana. This puts it well within the tropics. But if you think of Africa as having only thick jungles and vines, hot temperatures and dripping rain forests, you will change your mind. Africa is full of surprises, and here is one: much of Zimbabwe is high plateau and mountainous highland. That means that temperatures are moderate, with little jungle heat. In fact, the weather is very much like northern Califor-

Africa is a vast, exciting, mysterious place to many people.

nia's, with sunny days one after the other much of the year and nights that are cool and comfortable.

Almost everyone in Zimbabwe owns something warm to wear, like a sweater, a good jacket, or a thick shawl. But they do not own snow suits or ski outfits. Snow and bitter cold are things most Zimbabweans never experience. Because Zimbabwe is south of the equator, its winter is in July and summer in January.

Zimbabwe has great forests. They don't look much different than those in North America, except for two things: Zimbabweans have no pine trees in their forests, and North Americans have no baboons in their treetops!

The land is another surprise. Much of it is wide open, like the plains of the western United States. When Bulawayo was only a farming and ranch town, before it became the modern city it is today, it and the area around it were called the Bulawayo Range. The word "range" meant the same thing it meant to ranchers and cowboys in the Wild West: wide-open spaces where people and cattle could roam. The same is true in the north, around Zimbabwe's capital, Harare. In all directions outside Harare the same open range spreads.

Farming—and Rain

Zimbabwe is a rich land, blessed in many ways. When there is enough rain, it can produce great crops.

Many African nations cannot raise enough food to feed their people. Zimbabwe, in the good years, grows enough to sell to other countries. This gives it a great advantage in business.

Africans live very close to the land, and farming has always been very important. Wherever they lived or roamed through all the centuries for which there are no history books, African people laid out gardens. Some were family gardens. Others were large enough to feed whole villages. Large or small, these gardens represented *subsistence* farming—growing only enough to feed one's family or one's village.

Large-scale farming as a business was introduced to Zimbabwe by the whites who moved to it from South Africa at the end of the 1800s. Many found the land above the Limpopo to be fertile, so they staked out large farms and ranches—some a half-million acres in size. They grew many more crops than they themselves needed, and could sell their extra crops for cash. These large farms turned out to be highly successful. Zimbabwe grows tobacco, tea, sugar, cotton, coffee, citrus fruits, and groundnuts, a peanut-like plant. All are cash crops to sell to the country's own markets as well as to other countries.

When there is enough rain to soak the fields and fill the rivers and creeks, the crops stand tall and healthy in the farming land. If there is no rain, there is drought.

Zimbabwe's rich farmland can produce large cash crops, such as tobacco.

The rivers carry only dust, and then there is sadness, fear, and hunger in Zimbabwe and all of Africa. Plants no taller than a boot top turn brown and die in the gardens and the fields. It is then that villages begin to look empty and abandoned. The people who live in them go elsewhere, hoping to find some place where things will grow and people will not starve.

During times of drought, all who live in Africa look to the skies with great concern. This is when there are rain dances in the villages and prayers for rain in the churches.

Other Treasures

Underneath Zimbabwe's rich soil are more riches. Many of the most valuable and sought-after minerals in all the world lie underground in southern Africa. A belt of these treasures starts in South Africa, rises through Zimbabwe and Botswana, and runs northwest through Zambia and Zaire. Zimbabwe has important underground deposits of coal, tin, copper, gold, diamonds, nickel, chromium, asbestos, iron ore, and lithium. All these minerals play important roles in modern business and industry, and are in demand by the more advanced countries of the world. That means many customers for Zimbabwe.

This mineral wealth, combined with rich farmland,

means Zimbabwe is a very prosperous place, much more blessed, economically, than most of the other African nations. Yet, there is more.

Zimbabwe has many attractions, some made by nature and some by people. One of them is Victoria Falls, which is one of the great natural wonders of the world that people come from the corners of the earth to see. Another, less well known outside Zimbabwe, is the Matopos Hills region, south of Bulawayo. It is like a moonscape where leopards roam and where the great spirits (of whites as well as blacks) are said to gather. Then there is the Zambezi, one of the world's great rivers.

The Zambezi River rates with the Nile, the Niger, and the Congo rivers as among the most important in Africa and the greatest in the world. The Zambezi is 2,200 miles long and forms Zimbabwe's north and north-west borders.

At the westernmost corner of Zimbabwe, the Zambezi suddenly tumbles three hundred feet into a series of deep gorges. The water falls so far and hits the bottom with such force that its spray rebounds back up to the top and on into the sky.

This is Victoria Falls. The spray from the falls can be seen from forty miles away. Some days, when the clouds are low, the spray from the falls rises until it joins the clouds in the sky.

Beautiful Victoria Falls. When the sun shines, it is almost impossible to photograph the falls without getting a rainbow in the picture!

The first European known to have seen Victoria Falls was the Scottish missionary David Livingstone, one of the great white explorers of Africa. Livingstone was very impressed with the falls. He wrote in his diary that the angels must have circled back in their flight just to have a second look, so awesome is it all. Today tourists can fly over the falls in a light plane for a small charge. The airplane ride is named the Flight of the Angels, and taking it is a thrilling thing to do.

People can also hike to the edge of the falls, where they stand with nothing between them and the bottom. There is no fence or railing, and the rock at the edge is always wet and slippery. Most people are too nervous to stand at the edge, so they lie flat on their bellies and crawl to the edge to look over.

Mysteries and Marvels

Several hundred miles east of the falls is one of the world's new and exciting mysteries, the walled city called Great Zimbabwe. *Zimbabwe* means "stone enclosure" or "stone buildings"; Great Zimbabwe is a cluster of buildings, some in ruins and some still standing, that are very well-planned and well-built. The buildings hold clues to a highly organized, highly capable civilization that lived in the area long before whites settled here. Its builders are believed to be ancestors of Zimbabwe's Shona people. Like Victoria Falls, Great Zimbabwe draws many visitors who want to see it for themselves. This means a healthy tourist business for the country.

Farther upriver is another engineering wonder, Kariba Lake. It was formed when the Kariba Dam was built on the Zambezi River in the late 1950s to provide hydroelectric power for both Zimbabwe and its neighbor, Zambia. The people who had lived along the Zambezi for centuries were moved, and a great effort was made to drive wild animals to other areas before the land was flooded. Then the dammed-up water was allowed to spill over the land and the lake formed.

A large tourist area has been developed on the Zimbabwe side of the lake. The Zambezi is full of fish. Fishing and safari camps have sprung up on the shores of Kariba Lake, and its future seems promising. It is a fine area to view game. When the water ran over the land, it killed the trees. But the trunks of the trees still stand in the water, and many of Zimbabwe's unusual birds roost on them. There are many elephants in the area, and some of them find themselves in vacationers' pictures.

The Matopos Hills, which are directly south of Bulawayo, are much different in character. They may be unlike anything else in the world. The Matopos refers to twelve hundred square miles of granite columns, cliffs, and boulders that have been shaped by the winds of the centuries. Some of these formations are absolutely amazing. Great chunks of rock of different shapes and colors are stacked atop each other, as if some giant hand made something with a child's building blocks. Elsewhere, the Matopos look as if the same giant hand sprinkled the land with great boulders.

Both blacks and whites are drawn to the place. Great chiefs of long-ago peoples are buried somewhere here, and Africans believe their spirits still live in the

(Next two pages) *A view of the Matopos Hills.*

Matopos. Cecil Rhodes, who began the modern nation of Rhodesia, is buried here, too, on the top of a smooth hill. The Matopos is a shrine, for blacks and whites.

These are all geographical wonders. Zimbabwe's animals are living wonders. You will hear many wonderful stories, true stories, about the animals wherever you wander in Zimbabwe, because animals abound in Zimbabwe. Here's a list of just some of them: elephants, lions, leopards, buffalos, hippopotamuses, rhinoceroses, gorillas, chimpanzees, baboons, giraffes, gazelles, impalas, and lynxes. There are snakes and lizards of many varieties. Zimbabwe lists five hundred different birds, some with names like bee-eater, bishop bird, emerald cuckoo, and gray lourie.

Most of the animals are regarded as dangerous, and people assume that every snake is poisonous. Of all the animals, Zimbabwe's people are warned most often about the crocodile. It kills more people each year than any other animal, pulling them under when the people step into rivers to bathe, wash clothes, or swim.

Zimbabwe recognizes that its animals are part of its national wealth, and has set aside land in dozens of national parks, safari areas, and reserves. One of the most valuable is Hwange (once Wangy) National Park, near Victoria Falls.

Zimbabwe's animals are not as well known around the world as are those of Kenya and Tanzania, which are countries farther north in eastern Africa. Zimbabwe is trying very hard to spread the word of its animals, though, because travelers from other lands, particularly those from America and Europe, bring in money that Zimbabwe needs to buy things on the world's markets. If Zimbabweans can work together and end the differences that sometimes bring violence and frighten travelers away, its animals could become well known, too, for they are truly wonderful.

People — and Problems

By far, most of the people of Zimbabwe are black. In a population of more than eight million, fewer than 200,000 people are white. They all are open and friendly people. Most of them are tickled if strangers show interest in them and their land, and they will show people around with pride. Then they will want to know everything about their visitors and the places from which they come. Zimbabweans may live deep in the interior of Africa, but they are curious about the whole world.

The earliest inhabitants of Zimbabwe, as far as is known, were cave dwellers, thought to be Bushmen whose last descendants are found today in Botswana. The two main ethnic groups in Zimbabwe are the Shona and the Ndebele (sometimes called the Mashona and Matabele.) Both peoples were part of the great Bantu nation which migrated from the middle of Africa to its southern shore before A.D. 1000. First the Shona and then the Ndebele were forced north by the Zulu, fierce warriors of South Africa. Both settled north of the Limpopo River in Zimbabwe, where they themselves warred frequently. They never really joined together, as people of a country often do, and each looked down on the other.

In 1890 whites came, led by Cecil J. Rhodes, the British diamond billionaire for whom today's Rhodes Scholarships are named. The blacks thought Rhodes' Pioneer Column would merely pass through Zimbabwe on its way north, but the whites stayed. They built towns, laid out farms, and took firm control. They put down uprisings by the Shona and the Ndebele, who had gone to war to throw the whites out. The country was named Rhodesia, and whites, in connection with England, ruled it for ninety years.

When other colonies in Africa were turned over to majority, black rule following World War II, the Rhodesian whites refused to go along. They declared their independence from England, and a bitter, ugly civil war between blacks and whites began in Rhodesia, lasting thirteen years.

Finally, with blacks fighting a guerilla war and other nations refusing Rhodesian exports, the whites surrendered in 1980 and agreed to new elections; all would vote, black and white. A black prime minister, Robert Mugabe, was elected, and blacks took control of the new country they renamed Zimbabwe.

Many whites stayed. A lot of them had been born in Zimbabwe and loved it. Mugabe called for reconciliation, healing the divisions among Zimbabweans, and most people decided to give it a try. There were good rains the first year of the new government, and a bumper crop was harvested. Almost everyone took it as a good omen.

But it is easy to get along when times are good. Times became bad, and many people now worry about Zimbabwe. A terrible three-year drought killed crops and put fear in the people. Bad business situations like the recent recession meant less demand and lower prices for Zimbabwe's minerals.

And there is strain among the people. The old trouble between Shona and Ndebele returned. Mugabe, a Shona, had given a high place in the government to Joshua Nkomo, leader of the Ndebele. This cheered many people. Old enemies were going to work together. But when times turned bad, Nkomo was fired. Mugabe's supporters charged that Nkomo wanted to overthrow the Mugabe government. Nkomo fled, saying Mugabe's men wanted to kill him.

War flared up again. Some blacks, deserters from the army, roamed the bush, robbing and mistreating villagers. White farmers were murdered, and white tourists were kidnapped, never to be seen again. Each time something like this happened, the new country lost more of its white partners. They moved to places like Canada, Australia, and South Africa.

In October, 1984, rains fell again, good and heavy rains, and the whole country prayed they would last. They did, and by March, 1985, the government announced that the drought was over.

For the first time in three years, Lake McIlwaine, an important reservoir that was built to catch and hold water, overflowed its rim. So thrilled and grateful were the people that they gathered at the lake to watch the water spill over, and a drum and bugle corps played happy tunes.

But the rain did not ease all of the tensions in Zimbabwe. Prime Minister Mugabe called for another election, and the campaigning was violent. Mugabe said he wanted a one-party government, with all power reserved for his mostly-Shona party, and Nkomo and other black candidates fought this. The elections were finally held in July, 1985. Mugabe received an even bigger majority than in 1980. After the election he continued talking about a one-party Zimbabwe.

For the new country of Zimbabwe, rich and fertile and beautiful, the questions remains: can its people work together?

2. A Frontier People

The people of Zimbabwe, on whom so much depends, are usually among the warmest and friendliest on earth. It is not hard at all to talk to them. They are very open and honest people, just the sort you would expect to find on a frontier.

White and black, Zimbabweans take great pride in their country. They love it, and like nothing better than when someone from far away visits them and has a real interest in them. Then they show off their land proudly.

A teenaged black boy, eating a piece of fruit in the shade of the great council tree near Victoria Falls, is asked about the weather. The day happens to be almost perfect, with a spotless blue sky and warm sun. Is it true that in Zimbabwe every day is perfect? the boy is asked. His face breaks into a broad, beaming smile and he says, "Why, yes. Yes. Every day."

A white woman in Harare, her hair now fully gray, talks about what it was like thirty years ago, when much of the country was still undeveloped.

"The roads then weren't real roads like they are now," she said. "They were just two tire tracks in the bush grass. You aimed your car so the wheels were on the tracks and off you went. If you met another car

Tracks like this are sometimes the only roads through Zimbabwe's bush country.

coming the other way he'd be on the same tracks. So you would have to each drive off to the side and each take one track until you passed. You never knew whom you would meet on those tracks and you never knew what you would meet in the way of animals. Oh, then travel was an adventure! Every trip!

"This country was hard work in those days. It took a lot of hard work to make it what it is today. Real hard work, by everybody. But it was fun. Oh, yes, it was fun."

A black business owner in Harare greets his customers in a sporting goods store. Some of the customers are white and some are black. So are the clerks, some white and some black. The businessman says, "Yes, this is a good land. Everyone who has come here, from the first blacks to the earliest whites, has found it so. Can we work together to keep it so? That is our test."

There are many signs that Zimbabweans can get along in everyday life, if troubles between the races or among blacks are not stirred up. The two races—each regarding themselves as Africans together—play on sports teams together. They attend school together. They work side by side in stores and offices.

This matter-of-fact acceptance of each other is found everywhere, even though blacks only took their places on teams and in offices and stores a short while ago. The whites at store counters do not look uncomfortable, and the blacks behind the counters are among the most polite salespeople there are. They display no anger toward the whites, who regarded blacks as servants for a long time. The salespeople treat every customer, white or black, with courtesy and efficiency.

It would be incorrect, of course, to think that there are not racists—people who hate people of other races—

on both sides in Zimbabwe. Many whites resent black rule. Large numbers of whites left the country rather than live under a black government. Also, some blacks wish that all whites would leave, so that blacks could have the businesses and farms that whites still own.

As long as Zimbabwe's goal is to be a two-race nation where people are encouraged to get along with each other and to succeed together, the racists on both sides are a constant danger. Yet many whites and blacks in Zimbabwe today seem to treat each other with genuine respect and consideration. It is this acceptance that is the nation's great hope.

The Black Majority

Almost all of the people of Zimbabwe are black. They come from one of two large ethnic groups, the Shona or the Ndebele people, who often refer to their groups as tribes. Within each are other groups or clans that share the same language.

Most of Zimbabwe's blacks are descended from the great Bantu people, a super-nation that existed in Africa's earliest history and included many, many peoples. Historians say that one of the world's greatest migrations came when the Bantu people began to spread south from the Congo River, moving all the way to the tip of Africa and the Indian Ocean. From the Bantu

About 95 percent of Zimbabwe's people are black.

lands both the Shona and Ndebele moved to occupy lands south of Zimbabwe. At different times they would move north into Zimbabwe to stay.

The Shona (or Mashona) and the Ndebele (sometimes referred to as Matabele) were in Zimbabwe hundreds of years ago when national boundaries, as we see them today on the map of Africa, did not exist. Even today, though Zimbabwe and other African countries elect national governments, many Africans are loyal to their ethnic group or tribe before their government. Although all these groups are black, that is sometimes one of the few things they have in common. One often looks down on the other as second class. Groups bicker or fight with each other.

This was the case in Zimbabwe in the 1800s, before the white settlers arrived. The Ndebele and the Shona fought often, and were never really friends. The Shona were, and are, the more numerous group. But the Ndebele were more aggressive, more warlike. There was not much peace in the land when whites first came to Zimbabwe in 1890. In the long civil war of the 1960s and 1970s, Shona and Ndebele joined together to fight for majority rule. After the war was won, some of these old conflicts surfaced again.

Curiosity and Understanding

Today there is a lot of contrast among Zimbabwe's blacks. Some live in villages not much different than their ancestors' villages. These have mud huts, no artificial lights, and no running water. Water must be carried, and the only transportation for many is their feet. On the other hand, in the cities Zimbabwe's blacks are surrounded by everything that is modern.

The blacks in the cities wear business suits, not

An Ndebele woman in Victoria Falls.

traditional dress, when they are on the job, and blue jeans other times. The business people carry briefcases. Everyone speaks English, Zimbabwe's official language, and most of them do it with great skill.

What all the blacks share, whether they live in the cities or the countryside, is a deep curiosity about the world and a deep interest in people from other places. Villagers might be a little more shy and less quick with their questions, but the same interest is there.

It is not unusual for a black clerk in a store, or a villager you meet along a dusty road, to take what seems all the time there is to answer your questions. Africans are very eager that other people know who they really are and how they live. If you ask an African about the land and the people, you may be surprised at the direct, honest answers you receive. For instance, you might mention to an African that some people seem to be very poor, and he or she might reply, "Yes, Africa is very hard, but some make it harder because they do not help themselves."

Africans are like this. They don't dodge questions and they are free with their answers. Africans don't pretend to know what they don't know, either. Even though they may not be up on world affairs, they do seem to have an understanding of people that bridges the gaps in knowledge.

At Victoria Falls, an old market woman asked where her visitor was from, and then asked, "How is it in Detroit?" Told that many people were out of work, she said, "Ah . . . That is not good," and her face fell. This woman has never traveled out of a corner of Zimbabwe, yet she could relate perfectly to the suffering in Detroit.

This human understanding is found often among

many people of Africa. It is as if they know that the
world is shared by all people, no matter where the
people live and whether they ever meet. When you come
into contact with this understanding in Africans, it
seems like a beautiful and hopeful thing.

A common mistake, in talking about a frontier
(which is what Zimbabwe is today), is to picture only
white pictures; that is, pictures of white men in bush
shirts, prospecting for gold, building dams or tilling
great farms with their rifles nearby. Because if Zimbabwe is a frontier for its whites, it is quite the same for
its blacks. The leathery feet of an old black African who
has never worn shoes is as much a sign of the frontier as
are the beat-up hands of the white farmer who wrestled
the land until a farm was made. For all its richness, its
beauty, and its sunshine, Zimbabwe has been a rugged
place for both races.

The White Minority

In many ways, people are shaped by the kind of
land they live in. Zimbabwe's whites look like the sort of
people whom you would expect to find on a frontier.
They have an out-of-doors look, even when they are
dressed up in their finest for a party in the city. The fine
clothes can't hide the windburn and the sunburn that
come from working outdoors. The farmers can't dis-

Houses like this one are often found on the large farms of Zimbabwe.

guise their hands, which in mose cases have known real labor and show it with bumps and nicks. Zimbabwe's whites and their forebears carved modern farm businesses out of the African bush, and it was, and is, hard work. These are people who have lived a frontier life where, if you need a tool, you often have to make it, and then you have to be ready to repair it when it breaks.

Almost every white farm is the home of a family: husband, wife, and children. All but the smallest farms employ black workers and household help. The husband was almost always the farmer and overseer, while the wife usually supervised the household. But many unforeseen things happen on a frontier. In practice, the man could do the woman's work in the household. The women could pitch in where needed, too. Although things are much easier than when their mothers and grandmothers moved out to Africa, the women still must know how to drive the tractor as well as the car. Many of them know how to shoot a gun, if they need to. They have run schools on the isolated farms and they have served as both doctors and nurses on the bush ranches. Many of them have had to totally run farms or businesses when the men were away. They are frontier women still, capable, multitalented, and resourceful.

Today in Harare, some of the older women go to tea or go shopping dressed in flowery bonnets and white gloves to the elbow, but with many of them this is a disguise. Under that bonnet, in a lot of cases, is a grandmother who ploughed many a field (probably with a rifle by her side) when she and the country were younger.

Living Together

White explorers, missionaries, settlers, and fortune seekers have been in Africa since the 1600s, especially in

South Africa. In those times, some came to Africa for
religious freedom. Some came to farm the land. Others
came to see if the legend was true: wherever you dug a
mine in Africa you would find diamonds and gold.
Some were thieves and cheats. Others were adventurers
with great dreams.

All of them had one thing in common. They all
believed that if they crossed just one more mountain
range or forded just one more wild river, they would
find the perfect valley to settle in or a fortune beyond
their wildest dreams. In a way, they were like the great
roaming black clans. None of them could sit still for
long. The whites started the great farms and dug mines
to get at the minerals in the earth. They built dams and
roads, bridges and railroads. And they built cities that
look very much like North American cities.

Whites take great pride in what they and their
ancestors built in Zimbabwe. A white businessperson in
Bulawayo, brought to Zimbabwe from England when
he was just an infant, talks of the mines, the farms, the
highways, the railways, the dams, and he says, "I think it
is a remarkable achievement in just ninety years."

The blacks who have taken over the government
agree. There has been no move to destroy the things the
whites have built, but to keep them running and growing. It is official policy in Zimbabwe to encourage the
whites to stay, because their skills are badly needed.

For their part, blacks have taught the whites, too, in certain ways. The same businessperson told how his mother, who was very old, became senile and began acting like a young child again. It upset the household, and the man and his wife finally did not know what to do. But their African housemaid knew. In the village where she was born, a family stays together. There are young children in the family, and there are very old parents and grandparents. The maid said it was believed in the village that when people get very old they turned into children again. This was accepted in the village and no one became excited when an elder began to act like a toddler. The elder was allowed to be what he or she was, and life went on.

The maid took over the care of the old woman in the white home and treated her with exactly the care and respect the senile elders in the village received. Peace returned to the home. To the white man and his wife, it was as if it were magic. But it was just the simple wisdom from a so-called primitive village.

3. History in Black and White

Zimbabwe, like Africa in general, has two histories. The first is the centuries-old tales of native Africans and their wars and great migrations across the continent. The other has to do with adventurers, traders, and missionaries who nibbled at the two coasts of Africa from the earliest days of the great sailing explorations from Asia and Europe.

Written history tells us that, for hundreds of years after Columbus reached America and the first colonies were started there, Zimbabwe and the rest of the vast interior of Africa was a mystery land to outsiders. Arab and probably Chinese sailors, looking for gold and slaves, were the first outsiders to come to Africa. They sailed the Indian Ocean and covered the whole length of Africa on the east side. Europeans did not get much farther than the Mediterranean coast of Africa until the fourteenth and fifteenth centuries, when explorers like Columbus, Magellan, and the rest sailed to distant places. During those years, European ships explored the Atlantic coast of Africa, each ship trying to go a little farther. Finally, in 1488, Bartolomeo Diaz of Portugal became the first to sail around the southern tip of Africa, proving that Africa did end somewhere. Diaz

*Except for the coastal areas, southern Africa remained unex-
plored by Europeans until the sixteenth century.*

sailed on into the Indian Ocean and planted the Portuguese flag on the shores of Mozambique, Zimbabwe's neighbor to the east.

Almost every exploring ship carried missionaries and traders as well as soldiers. The traders sought out the strongest African peoples and made business arrangements with them. These whites traded cloth and manufactured goods in return for gold and slaves. Slavery was not new to Africans. Stronger groups had always taken slaves for themselves from people defeated in wars. Now they raided weaker peoples to supply slaves to the foreigners, who carried many of them to America and even more to Arab lands and the Orient. Eventually the foreigners were paying for slaves with firearms.

From the Africans with whom they did business, the traders and explorers heard fascinating tales of great kingdoms in the interior, kingdoms with unheard-of treasures in gold. Some of these lay across the Inyangi Mountains, the explorers were told, in what is today Zimbabwe.

Missionaries and gold seekers were the first foreigners, on both coasts, to try to get to the interior of Africa. They found it terribly hard going. Fevers and illnesses killed great numbers of them. So did wild animals and unfriendly Africans. Many simply disappeared into the interior, and no trace of them was ever found.

Meanwhile, Diaz's trip around the southern tip of the continent had opened the way for explorer fleets from Europe. In 1652, the Dutch East India Company established a station at Cape Town in what is now South Africa. The station was at the southernmost tip of Africa, and it was meant to be a place where Dutch ships sailing to and from China, India, and other places in the Orient could stop for fresh water and food. This was the first European settlement south of the equator in Africa. Eventually, the little settlement attracted more Europeans, and it began to spread out from Cape Town.

Fortune hunters moved north, looking for the same rich kingdoms the first explorers had heard tales of. Settlers sought more and more land. The fortune hunters and the settlers were determined to succeed, just like those Europeans on the coasts who earlier had tried again and again to get into the interior. No hardship was enough to turn gold and diamond seekers back if they thought they might become fabulously rich. The settlers were people who wanted space that would allow them to live as they wished. They searched for freedom in the same single-minded way others hunted for gold.

In the late 1800s gold was found in enormous quantity at Johannesburg and diamonds at Kimberly in South Africa. It seemed at last that some of the great tales of fortunes in the hard earth were true. A great many more Europeans hurried to South Africa to get their "share."

Whites Arrive in Zimbabwe

Even so, it was not until 1850 that Dr. David Livingstone, the Scottish missionary, became the first European we know of to reach the Zambezi River and get a look at Zimbabwe. Livingstone, on this first trip, followed the Zambezi into Mozambique, all the way to the Indian Ocean. On a second trip, some years later, he discovered the great falls on the Zambezi and named them for Victoria, queen of England.

Livingstone's diaries tell how difficult it was in the interior for whites. He writes of endless days on the trail in terrible heat and humidity, pestered constantly by insects that carried diseases, and attacked by animals and native people. Many in Livingstone's party died and were buried along the trails, including his wife. The survivors went on, never sure where the next step would take them.

Ten years after Livingstone's first trek into Zimbabwe, a discovery was made by an American named Adam Renders that continues to fascinate people today. Sometime in the 1860s, Renders stumbled on the ruins we now know as Great Zimbabwe. These are a series of stone buildings with walls around them, some

A statue of David Livingstone, one of the first Europeans to see Zimbabwe.

on hills and some on plains. They were of such size and magnificence that people assumed they were the capital of some great ancient kingdom. Clusters of buildings were surrounded by walls. The methods used to build these structures—countless slabs of stone perfectly balanced atop each other—amazed all who saw it. Birds carved in sandstone and mounted on these structures are now national art treasures. (Today these birds are pictured on Zimbabwe's flag.)

In 1871, Renders rescued another explorer, Carl Mauch, and later took him to see Great Zimbabwe. Mauch spread word of the great find and wondered aloud to others if Great Zimbabwe might not be the place of legendary riches, King Solomon's Mines. This talk spread among the fortune hunters already in the northern part of South Africa, and many of them hurried to Great Zimbabwe. They climbed the ruins and dug about them like crazed animals, finding no gold but sadly doing great damage.

One person who looked north with more than gold on his mind was Cecil Rhodes, who had come to South Africa from England in 1870 as a sickly teenager. Rhodes at first tried to farm cotton with a brother, but both were drawn to the gold fields. When a great field of diamonds was found near Kimberly, Cecil Rhodes went there and started digging. These were days when fortune hunters, high-born or low, could get rich if they worked hard enough and dared enough. Rhodes succeeded; by 1891, his company, the famous DeBeers Co., owned 90 percent of the world's known diamonds, and his fortune was immense.

Rhodes was a dreamer. He believed strongly in a British Empire, which then stretched around the world, and he believed that white Europeans were superior people and had to civilize other people. Rhodes dreamed of British territories and colonies stretching from the bottom of Africa at Cape Town to the top at Cairo, Egypt, and it became his dream to build a railway that whole length. Using his own money, he started working toward that dream.

His first stop was the land north of the Limpopo, today's Zimbabwe. In 1890, Rhodes organized a band of settlers, fortune hunters, soldiers, and explorers, and sent them north. In the history of Rhodesia and Zimbabwe, this band is known as the Pioneer Column. The Column, burying many members who died along the way, passed through many dangers in the south part of Zimbabwe and moved onto the great high plain. It continued north until it stopped near the Hunyani River, where a fort was built. The fort was called Salisbury, after Robert Gascoyne-Cecil, Marquesse of Salisbury, who was prime minister of England three times during the great days of the British Empire. Before long, Salisbury was capital of a new land, named Rhodesia after Cecil Rhodes.

Another History

All of this is white history. We know it quite well, because it is written in the journals of explorers, the diaries of missionaries, in government documents, and in books by the first writers on the scene. "Civilized" people write everything down and throw almost nothing away. But Zimbabwe has another history, the unwritten history of all the years before the whites came. This ancient black history was passed from one generation to another verbally, in stories or in songs, and wasn't written down. There remain many mysteries. The earliest inhabitants of Zimbabwe left paintings on the walls of caves, and these tell us something about how they lived. But they did not sign their paintings or leave anything that would tell us how they felt about things.

One of the exciting things going on today all over Africa, including Zimbabwe, is an energetic hunt for this mysterious unwritten history. Slowly, slowly what there is to find is being uncovered. One of the mysteries concerns the ruins of Great Zimbabwe.

For many years after whites first came to Africa, they called it "The Dark Continent." This was not just because the people of Africa were dark-skinned; it was also because they were "in the dark" about the modern world. The wheel had not been discovered in Africa at that time, and people there still did the hard labor of carrying or dragging things that had to be moved. Also, Africans worshipped things in nature—the sun, rivers, rocks, snakes—while the Europeans were mostly Chris-

A close-up of the finely constructed walls still standing at Great Zimbabwe.

tians and worshipped one God. The Africans didn't live the way Europeans did, so the Europeans judged the Africans as simple and inferior to whites.

For years, then, Europeans refused to believe that African blacks had built the city of Great Zimbabwe. They guessed that Arabs, or Chinese, or perhaps Hebrew people had put up those high walls and well-constructed buildings. Now, scholars generally agree that blacks did indeed build Great Zimbabwe. Research is being done to uncover other parts of Zimbabwe's unwritten history as well, trying to find evidence to verify the songs, stories, and legends that had been passed down through generation of Shona and Ndebele people.

Today we believe that people lived on Zimbabwe's high plateau as long as 22,000 years ago. These early people hunted animals and gathered wild plants to feed themselves as they roamed. They left behind wonderful cave paintings showing how they lived. Over the centuries small bands of people who herded animals and grew food for themselves came to settle on Zimbabwe's highlands. Before A.D. 1000, people had established small farming communities. Metal tools made by these people have been found—proof that the people there mined the metal they needed and worked the metal into useful forms.

By the eleventh century quite a few people were

living in the area we now call Zimbabwe. Scientists believe these were the ancestors of today's Shona people. Clusters of villages were ruled by kings. According to legends, these kings controlled all trade and headed up their armies. They also were considered high priests in religious ceremonies. There were often wars between kingdoms. These wars made victorious kings very wealthy; defeated villages had to send cattle as a tribute, or payment, to the winners, and the society looked upon their cattle the way Western countries do their money.

Many people believe these Shona people built the city of Great Zimbabwe. In the city were markets and warehouses, housing and royal palaces, and religious shrines. The Shona supreme being, Mwari, was worshipped here. People farmed just outside the city, and worked in nearby mines to supply metal for tools and decorations. It's also believed that trade was carried out with places as far away as the eastern coast of Africa. Gold, cotton cloth, ivory, and iron goods were traded for beads, brass goods, and cowrie shells. Cowrie shells were used as both decorations and money at that time.

Today many also think that over 20,000 Shona lived in Great Zimbabwe at one time. In the mid-1500s, though, people left the city. Growing crop after crop in the same soil had made the soil less fertile, and cattle had eaten too much of the grass around the city. With so many people, the city no longer had enough close-by supplies of trees for fuel, and even the mines had begun to be depleted. Since the people could not be supported on the land, the king and all his subjects moved away from the site. Great Zimbabwe was a holy place still, but a city no longer.

Legends say that from this large kingdom came three smaller kingdoms ruled by three chiefs: in the north and the east, Mutota led the Monomatapa kingdom; to the south was Togwa and his kingdom; and in the middle of Zimbabwe was Changa, whose kingdom came to be known as the Changamire. Eventually the Changamire took over the Togwa kingdom and became a rival of the Monomatapa.

In the late 1500s Portuguese traders contacted the Monomatapa king and got his permission to dig mines and trade in the kingdom. The Portuguese tried to take more and more power from the king and encouraged missionaries to work with the people. But the Portuguese lost most of their influence in the mid-1600s when Dombo, a Changamire king, took over the Monomatapa kingdom and threw them out. This united kingdom—the Changamire, the Togwa, and the Monomatapa—came to be called the Rozwi empire. (The Rozwi were Dombo's crack warriors; the name means "destroyer.")

Over the years the leaders of the Rozwi empire would become less powerful. In the 1800s another great chapter in African history began and had a lasting impact on this kingdom.

The Ndebele

About 1830, the Zulu, who live in what is now South Africa, began to transform themselves into a great empire under a new king, Chaka. Chaka was a genius. He developed a short stabbing spear called the assegai, which came to be feared by all his enemies, white and black. He invented new war tactics. Then he led his warriors in a campaign to conquer neighboring kingdoms. He defeated all the people who chose to fight and accepted the surrender of those who knew better. All were absorbed into his new empire, which stretched for hundreds of miles and which he ruled cruelly. Before long, Chaka and the Zulu dominated much of southeastern Africa. (The Zulu fought the white settlers, too, but in later years would be defeated by the British.)

The Ndebele, who are a force in Zimbabwe today, made up one of Chaka's armies. A chief named Mzilikazi was their leader. Mzilikazi was accused by Chaka of not turning over all the cattle taken from a defeated people, and Mzilikazi fled rather than fight Chaka. He took the Ndebele north. They first made their home south of the Limpopo, raiding and conquering in Chaka's manner, and then they moved into Zimbabwe, making their home near Bulawayo. The Shona were already living in the north of Zimbabwe, around the Harare area.

When Mzilikazi died, he was succeeded by Lobengula, and it was Lobengula who ruled when the white Europeans from south of the Limpopo came asking favors. Rhodes got to him first. Rhodes knew that the only whites Lobengula trusted were missionaries, so he sent the son of a missionary to Bulawayo to get Lobengula to sign a treaty of friendship. That signed, he asked for mining rights and he got them, too. Before Lobengula knew what was happening, Rhodes' Pioneer Column had entered the country, and Rhodes had the permission and blessings of the British Empire to develop this new colony.

Lobengula was not happy. The Ndebele fought to try to throw the whites out in 1893, and afterwards the Shona tried. But when these short wars ended, whites were in control in both north and south. For almost a century, until independence brought black rule in 1980, whites had their own way.

White rule meant exactly that. Whites took the best growing land to build their great farms. Voting laws were written to give blacks a chance to qualify as voters; however, the requirements were so high in terms of a person's income and level of educaton that few blacks qualified. In the cities, neighborhoods were segregated,

Two photographs of Salisbury (now Harare) as it looked in the
1920s. Cecil Rhodes planned wide streets so that large farmer
carts could turn around easily.

with separate areas for blacks. The police and army were integrated, but only whites could be top officers.

Whites employed many blacks, and it wasn't always a choice for blacks, although it was not technically slavery. To ensure that there would be enough black laborers for the mines and the farms, a law was passed that blacks had to pay a tax on the hut and land they occupied. However, they could only pay the tax in the settlers' kind of money, which meant blacks had to go to work in the mines or on the farms to get it. If the blacks were needed for longer times at the mines or farms, the tax was simply raised.

In spite of the hard work—and all of them had to work hard—it was a good life for the whites. Almost all of them could afford servants. In the good years, it was a rich country, and everyone could prosper.

White rule was not all bad for the blacks, in some ways. The terrible fighting and raiding between the Shona and Ndebele ceased, and both groups grew in number. They also grew rich in numbers of cattle, Africa's traditional measure of wealth. In addition, the whites introduced schools and modern medical care to them.

But of course, the blacks were not truly free, and had little say over their lives. They were governed by rules that were nothing like the customs they had. For farming they were moved to the second-best land. As for Africans in the cities, men were given temporary homes in separate, segregated sections of the town. Wives were not allowed to join the men in town. Instead, the women and their children often lived on remote land, growing small crops to feed themselves and depending on their working men to send them money.

When the winds of freedom blew through Africa and many other parts of the world following World War II, the whites of Rhodesia tried mightily to stand firm. They had worked hard in Africa and had achieved much. They had made a good life for themselves, and they fought as long as they could to keep control. But change was in the air, and eventually Rhodesia's whites had to turn over the country to the blacks, who called it Zimbabwe.

It took a long and terrifying war to bring this about.

4. Civil War and Independence

Would you be brave enough to stand guard over your farm house at night with an adult's rifle while your parents got some sleep? If your village was burned, could you lead younger children to safety in the fields, living off melons and roots, sleeping on the ground?

Children had to do both during the war that led to Zimbabwe's independence. Everyone was involved in the war, men and women, children and grandparents, black and white, and almost no one was out of danger. Many were killed.

We usually think of war as two armies, each in its own uniform, fighting and dying. Of course, people who live in war-torn countries are killed and made homeless, too. But in war, as we usually think of it, soldiers are the ones who take most of the risks. However, the Rhodesian civil war was different. The black armies that fought to overthrow the white government were never big enough to battle the Rhodesian Army face to face, so they fought another kind of war, called guerilla war.

Guerilla war has been used throughout history by people with small armies—by the Israelites fighting the Syrians in ancient times; by Viet Cong Communists against both French and American forces in Viet Nam; and by both sides in Nicaragua and El Salvador most recently. Guerilla war is sneak, strike, and disappear. The object of it is not to capture cities or great sections of the countryside; rather, guerilla fighters frighten citizens and spread panic until normal life is totally impossible and the government collapses. Rhodesia, with its long, unguarded borders and its farms and villages dotting the broad range, was perfect for this sort of war.

In Rhodesia, black guerillas put exploding mines in roads and blew up rail lines and bridges. Two airliners were even shot down. They killed farmers and burned farm houses. They ambushed cars and killed the people in them. Schools were set afire and missionaries killed. Guerillas planted bombs in city stores and restaurants. They attacked tourist hotels. They raided villages and burned the crops. If other blacks insisted on going to their jobs at white farms or mines, they became enemies of the guerillas, too, and were terrorized and killed.

Every raid, bomb, and ambush had the same goal: to make life in Rhodesia so terrible that the whites would give up. If mines and farms could not ship their products because the bridges were blown up, the roads were unsafe, and too many black workers stayed home out of fear, the economy would suffer and the government would be weakened. If tourists were afraid for their lives, they would stay away and hurt business fur-

Almost everyone was involved in the war for independence in Zimbabwe. This militiaman had to guard the entrance to a village.

ther. If enough white farmers were murdered, the rest might flee. If children died in the raids on the farms, too bad, but that would spread even more terror. If enough villages were burned and enough villagers slain, the rest might be forced to flee to the cities, where the government would have a difficult time feeding them. If enough missionaries (who ran most of the schools and hospitals in the bush) were murdered, the rest would have to leave, and disruption would spread. If there was enough terror, the war might be won.

Freedom is often the goal of a guerilla war, and freedom is a good thing. But the means of getting it, as in Rhodesia, can be terribly ugly.

Beginnings for War

How did the Rhodesian civil war start? It started with the impatience of black political leaders to run their own land, and the stubborn refusal of the whites to truly share the good things they had made for themselves in Africa.

World War II, fought between 1939 and 1945, brought change to Africa. In World War II Germany took over almost all of Europe, and Japan conquered much of Asia and the Pacific, each making lands and people prisoners. The free world, where people could vote their leaders in and out of office and decide how to live their lives, was rapidly shrinking. Two of its leaders, America's Franklin D. Roosevelt and England's Winston Churchill, called on their peoples to fight back. They said freedom must be defended—for all. They dedicated their own efforts and the blood of their brave soldiers to saving freedom for all those under the control of someone else.

Africa (and all the other colonies of the world) heard these words and took them to heart. Almost all of Africa, before the war, lived under European colonial rule: French, German, Portuguese, and British. In almost no corner of Africa did black Africans make their own decisions, elect their own leaders, or write their own laws. Yet African blacks were asked to help save democracy and freedom during World War II. One famous fighting unit of that war was the King's African Rifles, also called the Rhodesian Rifles. There were many black Africans in its ranks, and it fought bravely in Burma against the Japanese.

When the war ended, Africans looked again at their own situations and decided they, too, should have some of this freedom the war had been fought over. At the same time—and this is very important—the war left most European countries battered, tired, and broke. The Europeans had to rebuild their own homes and could spare little attention or money for their colonies. The colonies, in some cases, were regarded as a burden.

India, Britain's great Asian colony, became independent in 1947, and soon it was Africa's turn. In 1957, the British colony known as the Gold Coast, located on the western shore of Africa, was set free. It was renamed Ghana and came under the rule of a magnetic black president named Kwame Nkrumah, who traveled the world urging other colonies to get their freedom.

In 1960, freedom roared through Africa like a wild fire. Fifteen former colonies became independent in 1960 alone, and more in 1961 and 1962. By 1964, all of Britain's African colonies were free, including Rhodesia's neighbors and trading partners, Northern Rhodesia and Nyasaland, renamed Zambia and Malawi.

Now it appeared to be Rhodesia's turn, and blacks who had been working for independence there were impatient. But Rhodesia was different. Other British colonies in Africa, like Ghana and Nigeria, had been governed by English people who never thought of Africa as their home. England was their home, and always would be. These British subjects would come to Africa for five or ten years to run a colony for the Queen, but they always went home. They were English.

Rhodesia's whites, however, saw themselves as Africans. Yes, England was where most of them had come from, but they had sunk deep, personal roots in Africa. They had built homes and cities, and their children had been born in Rhodesia. They had no intention of going back to England, and they refused to surrender control of Rhodesia's government to the blacks, even though the blacks outnumbered them thirty to one.

When England urged Rhodesia's whites to give way before the tide of freedom in Africa, the whites refused. On November 11, 1965, Rhodesia's white prime minister, Ian Smith, issued a proclamation called the Unilateral Declaration of Independence, or UDI, declaring Rhodesia independent of England and everyone else. Then the whites prepared to fight majority rule any way they could.

It is felt that this UDI triggered the long war in which many died, and it is a very sore spot still. If you are a white person in Zimbabwe today and your birthday falls on November 11, you do not celebrate on that day. You celebrate the day before or the day after. If you hold your party on November 11, someone is likely to think that you are celebrating UDI, and there could be trouble.

The UDI enraged black activists. They planned riots and called for strikes. They picketed at the bus stations to keep black workers from going to work in white businesses, and they threw stones at the buses. The white government struck back firmly. Police fought with and scattered the rioters, killing some. Black leaders were arrested and taken to camps in remote areas of the country, to keep them from causing more trouble.

The government sent troops into the bush to hunt for the guerillas.

But freedom was in the air, and it could not be bottled up so easily. The protests continued. Acts of violence became more frequent. Weapons were buried in the countryside by blacks, where they could be dug up when needed. On the white side, every riot and every fight made the government more determined to resist.

In April, 1966, the first major armed clash took place between blacks and Rhodesian soldiers at Sinoia, west of Salisbury (Harare), and the war was on.

The fighting was not exactly black against white. The army which fought to defend the white government included many blacks. So did the special police forces which were sent into the bush to hunt down guerillas. The two guerilla armies who fought the government did not have the support of all the country's blacks, and their armies were rather small. One guerilla army, under Joshua Nkomo, operated from Zambia. Another, under Robert Mugabe, was based in Mozambique. Nkomo and Mugabe were rivals for power, although they teamed up against the whites in the war. Nkomo's fighters would cross the Zambezi River by night, spend days or weeks attacking targets in Rhodesia, then slip back into Zambia. Mugabe's men came in across the mountains from Mozambique and did the same things.

The army, which had airplanes, helicopters, and military vehicles, chased the guerillas in the bush and attacked them in their safe camps in Zambia and Mozambique. Cruel acts were committed by both sides. Little fighting was done in or near the cities, although bombs were set off in Bulawayo and Salisbury, and a giant oil fire was set in Salisbury. There were too many troops in the cities for the guerillas to risk battle there. Most of the fighting was done in the outlying areas

Everyone, black and white, suffered during the war. This woman's daughter was a flight attendant on an airliner shot down by guerillas.

where, of all Rhodesians, black villagers probably suffered the most. They were caught in the middle. The government passed laws that anyone who aided the guerilas would be put to death. The guerillas regarded villagers who refused them help as supporters of the whites and would kill them. Nkomo and Mugabe claimed that many of the terrible acts blamed on guerillas were actually done by black soldiers. These soldiers, they said, wore everyday clothes to make them appear to be guerillas.

Thousands of both races died. Many black Rhodesians fled the country to avoid the war, and so did some whites. But there was great will on both sides. The guerilla leaders felt sure freedom would be theirs if they fought on. They took more and more young blacks to Zambia and Mozambique for training as fighters.

The whites refused to give up. Whites trained their children to use guns and ordered grandfathers into the army. They fitted the bottoms of their cars with armor to protect the passengers from land mines, and they struggled to keep the farms and mines going.

The war lasted thirteen years. Meanwhile, another kind of conflict was going on, in the area of world opinion. To gain support of other countries, each side in Rhodesia publicly accused the other of cruelty after cruelty. The blacks won this "war" easily. The United Nations declared the white government of Rhodesia illegal and asked all countries to stop trading with it. The United States came out for black rule, and so did the Soviet Union, which supplied Nkomo's guerillas with training and weapons. Other Communist countries aided Mugabe's armies. More and more, the white government of Rhodesia had no friends among other

Joshua Nkomo (above left), *Bishop Abel Muzorewa* (above right), *and Robert Mugabe* (below) *led various black political parties during and after the civil war.*

nations and was under added strain. Finally, in 1979, it tried to arrange black rule itself: it made an agreement with a black leader not involved in the war, Bishop Abel Muzorewa. Muzorewa would become prime minister, and the country would be called Zimbabwe-Rhodesia.

But this move was made too late. Nkomo and Mugabe said that unless they and their people were included in the new government, they would keep fighting. The United States sided with the guerillas and called Zimbabwe-Rhodesia a fraud. So did other countries.

At this, the white government fully gave in and agreed to meet in London, England with the guerillas to make another arrangement. Out of this came a new constitution, under which blacks vote freely. Robert Mugabe, whose people, the Shona, are more numerous, won election as prime minister. The whites were granted twenty seats out of one hundred in the House of Representatives, even though whites do not make up twenty percent of the population.

On April 18, 1980, Rhodesia was no more. It became the free and independent Republic of Zimbabwe.

As prime minister, Mugabe surprised many people when he made room for his rival in the election, Joshua Nkomo. It seemed that Shona, Ndebele, and whites would work together in the new country.

After independence, black and white Zimbabweans tried to live in peace—something children seem to know how to do.

But the old division of Ndebele set against Shona, of Mugabe against Nkomo, continued, and put a shadow on Zimbabwe's future. When Nkomo left the new government after a dispute with Mugabe in 1982, some of his supporters who had fought as guerillas deserted from the army and took their weapons with them. Tourists were kidnapped. Farmers were slain once again. Roads became unsafe. When Mugabe sent troops into the bush to hunt down the deserters, it was as if the war were starting again. Villagers once more looked with fear at the appearance of armed strangers.

The violence spilled over into politics, too. In the elections scheduled for 1985, some people running for office were murdered. Joshua Nkomo and Bishop Abel Muzorewa both challenged Robert Mugabe in the election for prime minister. Mugabe held a meeting of his party and pushed hard for its becoming the only political party in Zimbabwe, a change many people disagree with. Mugabe won a majority in the election and another five-year term.

Zimbabwe's greatest hope and asset is its people. The ways in which blacks and whites have learned to live with each other in this rich African country gives everyone hope that all in Zimbabwe will settle disagreements and find peace.

5. *Stories, Spirits, and Celebrations*

Africa's legends tell the stories of all the centuries: of great migrations, strong kings, and nations that disappeared. They also tell about animals, the land around a village, spirits, and magical happenings. Stories are important to black Zimbabweans and to black Africans in general. In each ethnic group's set of stories are found the history, customs, or common worries of their people. The stories are also wonderful entertainment for everyone.

What sort of stories do Africans tell? Often there are poems and songs that praise old kings and tell of old wars. This sort of story gives hints about the history of Zimbabwe. But, no one can ever quite know if a story is actually history or the "official version" of a long-dead king, who made up the story to tell people that he was richer or braver than he was! Sometimes, several versions of the same story exist; then, people who write down history have to try to unravel the puzzle of which one is true.

Other stories remind listeners of rules and customs—but they do this in a very clever way. Often the main characters of the stories are animals or mythical creatures such as giants. These creatures stand for real

The Zimbabwe bird, atop this monument, today is a symbol of Zimbabwe's unwritten history, preserved only in story and song.

human beings. One type of character that often appears in African stories is called a trickster. Often, a hare is cast in this role. The trickster uses lies, tricks, or magic to get what he or she wants, but in the end winds up losing everything gained by these methods. The trickster shows people what *not* to do. Here is one such story likely to be told:

A drought has fallen on the land. All the animals except Hare work to build a well so that they might have water to drink. After the well has been built, Hare scares off the others with a loud noise and has the well to himself. While he is there he gets the water in the well dirty when he bathes in it. Soon the other animals figure out who scared them and decide to punish Hare. They build a sticky "animal" figure and stand it up next to the well. When Hare arrives, he orders the animal to leave, which of course it does not. Hare then tries to hit and kick the creature and becomes hopelessly tangled and stuck on it. The other animals arrive and beat up Hare, then let him go. Hare runs into the grass in fear. That is why, to this day, hares and rabbits are frightened creatures and run away.

Besides being just a good story, the Hare tale tells villagers that everyone needs to share in the work and that greediness will be punished. The story also reflects some concerns of people who live in the bush: Will we be able to find enough water, and enough food, to live? Will the members of my village help each other when help is needed?

Although the occasions for storytelling vary, singing, dancing, and pantomime are often a large part of the telling. Usually, people in a village know the storyteller's legend, so a storyteller must sing and act out the story to keep it interesting for his or her audience. The storyteller also involves the audience by teaching them the chorus of a song or asking for help in acting out the story. Sometimes a story ends with a question so that

Music is often a big part of a storyteller's performance.

the ending can be debated and decided by the audience.
African people see the stories as an important part of
their lives, something to take heed of and feel, something that surrounds them.

Spirits All Around

This sense of living stories is shown in other ways as
well. Many Africans believe that there are gods who

watch over those who pray to them. Others believe that spirits choose to protect certain people from harm and give them special powers. Many also believe that the spirits of dead ancestors are still on the earth and have a lot to do with good and bad luck.

Missionaries who came to Zimbabwe worked hard to change these beliefs. They baptized many Africans over the years. In 1980, 58 percent of Zimbabwe's people declared themselves to be Christians. Of these, one-third said they were Protestants, a quarter said they belonged to African Christian churches, and a quarter of them said they were Catholics. There are also several Jewish congregations in Harare and Bulawayo. In addition, small numbers of people (less than one percent of the population each) are members of the Muslim, Hindu, and Bahai religions.

These numbers are impressive. But many missionaries will openly say that most Africans do not give up their traditional gods when they adopt yours. They simply add yours to theirs. Africans are comfortable with the idea of many gods. The more of them one honors, perhaps, the better one's chances.

Africans often pray to gods who can help them in their work. People who fish pray to the god who can send many fish into their nets. Hunters will beseech the gods of the forest to look kindly on them. Boat captains will pray to the river gods, so the gods will not tip over their boats. (Passengers often pay captains a little something extra, so they will say a very sincere prayer.)

Young women hope the gods will let them bear many children. A large family is a status symbol in much of Africa. Young women may pay close attention to a nurse's lecture on birth control, because too many people is often one of Africa's problems. But then, just like their mothers and grandmothers, they will go to a sacred rock, chip off a sliver of it, and wear it somewhere on their bodies for luck in having children.

Africa is one of the most spiritual places in the world. Almost everybody prays seriously to someone or something. Perhaps this is because the land can be so difficult and dangerous. Africans depend on the land for life itself—food and water. Living on such open land puts villages in danger from droughts, floods, terrible storms, and epidemics of sicknesses. The winds in Africa, for instance, can blow so strongly that they turn big birds around in the air and take a village's garden many miles away. Africans know, better than most people, that they are but specks in the path of forces like these and need all the help they can get.

Good Luck, Bad Luck

Some Africans believe that spirits will seek out certain people and make them luckier than most. Let's say you are sleeping on the ground when a snake slithers up to you. If it gets under you and curls up in the warmth of your body, but does not hurt you, some people will think of you ever after as the snake boy or the snake girl. They mean that you are in harmony with the snake spirits, which told that snake not to bite you. If your village is ever threatened by snakes, you will probably be expected to do something about it, because it is known that the snakes are your friends.

If you catch more fish than anyone else, you are the fish man, and others will probably want to cast their nets near yours to see if your luck rubs off on them. The same is true if you are a particularly fortunate hunter, or if your garden grows better than anyone else's, or if your cattle and your goats are fatter.

Spirits affect other Africans, too. Many people believe that the way things go for them depends on the moods of their own ancestral spirits, their dead mothers and fathers, aunts and uncles, or grandparents. Africans say that instead of going to Heaven, the spirits of dead family members stay nearby, keeping an eye on things.

People believe that if the spirits feel properly respected by those still alive, they shower the living with good luck and wonderful rewards. These rewards can mean good health, wealth, or protection from troublemakers. But if the spirits feel neglected, they can unleash terrible troubles on the disrespectful. They can make babies

sick, crops die, or cattle weak. They can send storms and winds, or enemies who will rob and kill.

There is no limit to the good and the bad Africans believe ancestral spirits can do, so they work very hard to keep them happy. There are ceremonies to honor them, with dances and song. Meals are set out for them. Corn is pounded into a rough flour and made into cakes which are called mealies. Often the best of the mealies are left for the spirits, so the spirits won't turn on the living.

Ancestor worship continues today in Zimbabwe, even though more and more Zimbabweans are educated in schools. Some people certainly have given it up, but deeply held beliefs of great importance are not easily rubbed out. It takes place today in the modern cities as well as in the bush.

Also, spirits of the great kings and chiefs hover constantly near their burial places, it is believed. Great Zimbabwe and the other ancient ruins in Zimbabwe, according to some scholars, were built partly as grand (and very respectful) homes for these big spirits. It is why these ruins became shrines as well as monuments.

Celebrating

Holidays are major occasions in Zimbabwe. They are celebrated with much enthusiasm and ceremony. It

An African legend says that once when the gods were angry at Africa, they pulled up all its trees and replanted them upside down!

is probably only natural for people who live on a frontier to celebrate seriously. Life is hard, often a struggle for survival. For many Africans of both colors, every day is a new challenge. When the opportunity comes to let loose for a day and celebrate, no one goes at it half-heartedly.

Our West was like that, too. The hoedowns and the harvest celebrations were full of meaning, and they were celebrated with great enthusiasm.

Zimbabwe celebrates a mixture of holidays. Some celebrate change in Zimbabwe and Africa. Others are old, traditional holidays brought to Africa by white people. Zimbabwe's newest holidays, the ones added to the calendar after independence, are all political holidays. The big moments on Africa Day, May 25, or Independence Day, April 18, are the mass rallies.

Enormous crowds of people gather in stadiums or parks to hear political leaders like Robert Mugabe remind them of the struggle to be free from colonial rule, to be free to work out one's own life. On these great black holidays, Mugabe and other leaders look down from the speaker's stand at an ocean of faces.

There are parades, parties, and dances. Vendors move through the great crowds selling treats. There is music everywhere, either live bands or recorded music, most of it stirring patriotic songs.

Africa Day celebrates a dream. The dream is that a

free black Africa can work together in brotherhood and sisterhood to better the lives of all its human beings. Brotherhood and sisterhood are hard work. They don't come easily, and there are many squabbles between African countries, even though almost all are led now by blacks and almost all are free. But Africa Day is set aside to remind everyone that, difficult as it may be, a friendly Africa working together is still a good goal.

On Africa Day, the huge audiences are also reminded that all of Africa is not yet free. Namibia, to the west of Zimbabwe, is still under the rule of South Africa, even though the United Nations has declared this illegal. And South Africa itself is still ruled by a minority of whites who refuse to allow its millions of blacks to take any part in running that country.

School is out on Africa Day. Schoolchildren are often involved in some of the parades and put on their own little ceremonies. Mines, stores, and factories are closed. Everybody celebrates.

The speeches at the rallies go on and on. American audiences might get restless. But Africans love speeches, and they expect their leaders to give good, long ones. The sun is hot, but speeches are a big part of African holidays, so no one seems to mind.

The black government of Zimbabwe is a Marxist government, which means it follows the teachings of Karl Marx, one of the foremost teachers of Commu-

Crowds often listen to long speeches on special days.

nism. Government and party officials in Zimbabwe call each other comrade. When their names appear in the country's newspapers, the letters "Cde." appear before their names. That's short for comrade.

Almost all countries with Marxist governments have big celebrations on May Day, May 1. In Zimbabwe, this is called Workers' Day. Marx taught that the workers should own everything, and thus be their own bosses.

The traditional national holidays in Zimbabwe are those that many Americans celebrate: Christmas, New Year's, and Easter. Then there are two others which are not national holidays in the United States: Boxing Day and Whitsunday.

Boxing Day is a British tradition, carried around the world in the days of the British Empire. Boxing Day falls on the first weekday after Christmas. It is simply the day when it is traditional to hand a Christmas box to the mail carrier, the newspaper carrier, and the delivery person.

Whitsunday is what U.S. Christians call Pentecost, celebrated on the seventh Sunday after Easter. In the United States it is celebrated in church on Sunday, but in Zimbabwe it is a grand holiday, lasting two days.

On Sunday, there are special church services that feature old customs that the ancestors of white Zimbabweans brought to Africa with them. One ancient custom is decorating the churches with branches and scattering flowers on the church floors.

It is a happy time. Whitsunday also features dramas, dances, and special foods, especially sweets. Some say one must wear only brand-new clothes on Whitsunday if one is to have good luck the following year. Farmers think that if the weather is good on Whitsunday there will be a big harvest.

No one works or goes to school the Monday after

Whitsunday in Zimbabwe. The holiday goes on through Monday. It is a good time for Zimbabweans to take trips, since it is a two-day holiday. Those who can afford it sometimes plan Whitsunday trips across the country or even into neighboring countries such as Malawi, with its lovely lake. It is a good time, too, for Zimbabweans who work in the cities to travel back to their home villages for visits.

In church, Whitsunday celebrates the moment when the Holy Ghost descended from heaven to encourage the apostles to carry the word of Jesus Christ to every corner of the earth. On Whitsunday, the Holy Ghost gave the apostles the gift of tongues, so that they could speak many languages and thus be understood by many people.

Whitsunday seems perfect for Africa. People who believe that the spirits of their own ancestors hover about every day, watching what the living are up to, must be very comfortable with the idea of the Holy Spirit suddenly appearing in the sky.

6. City Living

You have to wait for the green light before you cross one of the wide downtown streets in Harare, the capital of Zimbabwe. Harare may be deep in the heart of Africa, but in many ways it is as modern as this minute.

This is another of Africa's surprises. Africa still consists of hundreds and hundreds of square miles of open, wild bush country. But set down in the open range are cities that compare favorably with any in the world. Harare is one of the nicest in Africa, clean and well run. So is Bulawayo. Zimbabweans are proud of both of them.

You can catch a bus in Harare, buy a pizza, and then eat your dinner in a green park. People dress pretty much the way Americans do, including the children. Downtown Harare is full of shops, department stores, and office buildings, and there are even a few small shopping malls. Most people live in suburban districts, where a lot of the homes are one-story houses with driveways.

There are always reminders that this is Africa. It might be someone in traditional costume or someone in rugged bush clothes. It might be a Land Rover, the heavy-duty vehicle designed to be driven where there

Downtown Harare has a low and open look.

are no roads. It might be the dwarf deer in your garden, eating your rosebuds when you aren't looking.

If you drive to the top of the *kopje*, or hill, where a flame is kept burning to honor the memory of Cecil Rhodes' Pioneer Column, you can see the countryside spreading out from Harare, and that will remind you this is Africa. But in a downtown cafe, on one of the shopping streets, or in one of the excellent hotels you would be forgiven for thinking you were in a middle-sized English or American city.

Looking at the City

Far more Zimbabweans live in the countryside than in the two main cities or the smaller cities around the country. Harare's population was estimated at 656,000 in 1982; Bulawayo's is about a third of that.

Harare is the center of government and home to the main university and the national library and museum. It is a bustling place. Africa is full of wide open spaces, but on the sidewalks of downtown Harare there are so many people out and about on weekdays that "Excuse me" and "Pardon me" are heard all the time.

Western clothes are worn by just about everyone. Government officials and businessmen of both races are almost always dressed in suits, shirts, and ties. Businesswomen wear dresses or suits with dressy shoes.

People in Harare dress much as Americans do.

Young people wear jeans-type pants whenever they can, with T-shirts. But young people who work in the stores and shops dress up a little for work. The young men wear neat dress shirts behind the counters, not T-shirts, and young women in shops wear blouses. There is no dress code; rather, there seems to be a sense that certain jobs require nicer clothes. Some schoolchildren wear uniforms. Others, whose schools give them free choice, wear pants and shirts or simple little dresses called shifts. Because the weather is like California's, you don't see a jacket or a topcoat very often. Most women will carry a sweater or shawl when they're out in the evening.

Traditional African dress is rare on the streets of Harare or Bulawayo. For one thing, the striking, many-colored costumes and headpieces sometimes pictured in travel magazines are usually for special occasions like festivals. They are not suitable for everyday wear, particularly for a day's work. Also, Western dress is modern, and Zimbabweans are eager to show the world that they belong in modern times.

It is much more common in the cities to see traditional British Empire dress. The most frequent example of this is khaki dress shorts, knee socks, and a bush shirt with epaulets, or shoulder straps, on the white men. This was the standard "uniform" for centuries for men who went out from England to India, Egypt, and Africa to run the empire.

Mornings

Zimbabwe is an early-to-rise place. Pioneers on the frontier got going early in the morning. They had much to do and, before electricity, they had to do it all by the light of the sun. Zimbabwe's cities and towns are well wired today for artificial light, but the habit of early-up has carried over.

A common breakfast for black Zimbabweans in the city, children included, might be corn bread and a cup of tea. Just about everyone drinks tea in Zimbabwe. English Zimbabweans have a pot brewing at all times, and if they have to go on a drive that will take more than a half hour, they take along a thermos. Blacks drink tea almost as often as the whites.

An English breakfast is likely to be a bigger meal than a black Zimbabwean (or the average American in a hurry to get going) would eat. Double breakfast is an English custom. English people take a cup of tea and a roll upon getting up, then go off to clean up and dress. When they are ready for the day, they sit down and eat a second breakfast: eggs, toast, marmalade, bacon, sausage, fruit. If you aren't English, it sounds like a lot, but to an English man or woman it's the only way to start the day.

Everyone who can afford a car drives to work, and many children are driven to school. French cars seem most popular today in Zimbabwe, particularly the Peugeot. There are American cars, too, although not many. For those who can't drive, there are public buses as well as school buses and taxicabs, and it is easy to get around Zimbabwe's cities.

Many of Zimbabwe's schools still are not public schools. Rather, they are religious or private schools, although by law they must be open to all who qualify. Unlike America, there are not schools in every neighborhood. Even young children must be driven to a far-away school or must sometimes walk quite a distance.

Industry in the cities is often located in special areas that are like industrial parks. But downtown is the center of the action, particularly in Harare. Downtown is where the government offices are, as well as big stores and offices of major businesses.

Downtown Harare is crowded with all the different faces of Africa. Many visitors come to Harare because it is the capital and the center of business, and so you can stand on a street corner and see people of Europe, Asia, and America pass by.

Shopping in Harare is international-feeling, too: there are things to buy from all over the world. The main reason for this is that many different people from different lands came to Africa to explore and do business. Many stayed and opened businesses, and their shops still reflect their homelands. A good example is the Indians, who settled into businesses all up and down the east coast of Africa and in Zimbabwe. A lot of people are surprised to learn that a number of Italians also settled in Zimbabwe.

Stores sell goods from many countries in downtown Harare.

Some American goods can be found in Harare's stores, although European goods are much more common. Imported goods only trickled in for many years. During the world recession of the early 1980s, the prices Zimbabwe was paid for its mineral exports fell, and it was unable to buy many foreign goods from anywhere. In Zimbabwe's case some difficulties, many stemming from the worldwide boycott of Rhodesia in the 1970s, have turned out for the best. For example, Rhodesia used to import almost all its personal clothing from

Homes in some townships are simple but sturdy.

England, but when political and economic difficulties cut off the shipments, Rhodesia began making its own clothing. Today Zimbabwe has a thriving, growing clothing industry that makes many jobs for people and exports clothing to other countries.

Suburban Living

By early evening, except for restaurants and clubs, downtown stores are closed and people have returned to their homes in the residential districts, called suburbs or townships in Zimbabwe.

The nicest residential areas were for whites only during white rule. Blacks lived in separate townships. Under the black government, that is changing. Black professionals and government officials who can afford better homes have integrated the best areas. Many neighborhoods have both black and white residents today, while some neighborhoods are still mainly black or mainly white. The difference is that no one is kept out of any area anymore by law. Today anyone can live anywhere he or she can afford.

The homes in better areas are almost identical to American homes. They have electric lights, modern stoves and refrigerators, indoor plumbing, and, with some, attached garages. A Zimbabwean house could be moved into an American neighborhood and no one would notice much difference.

There usually is more land around a Harare or Bulawayo home than around U.S. suburban homes. Zimbabwean cities just don't seem as tightly packed. Perhaps this is because there is so much room in Africa that everyone can spread out a little. Many homes have sizable gardens out back. Vegetables grow well in Zimbabwe's climate.

A lot of homes have living quarters for house servants. There are many people seeking jobs in Zimbab-

Many people take jobs as household helpers. This nanny cares for these children during the day.

we, and household work is not looked down on. One of the first things the black government did when it took office was to require a minimum wage, and that raised the pay of maids and gardeners as well as miners, farm workers, and shopworkers. Even so, most families with an average income can afford household help. Both black and white Zimbabweans have help, not just the very rich.

Houses are smaller in the neighborhoods where those less well-off live, as is true around the world. In the poorer neighborhoods of Zimbabwe, and in the old black townships of Harare and Bulawayo, many of the houses are of cement block and not fancy. But they are solid and much better than houses in poor sections of other African countries, where many people live in unsanitary and unhealthy shacks.

High Tea and Wood Fires

Some people still practice the old English custom of afternoon tea. In this instance tea means a light meal in the late afternoon that is meant to keep people from starving before they get dinner. Little sandwiches (sliced cucumber on white bread is traditional and delicious) or little cakes are served with cocktails, coffee, or tea.

A landmark in Harare is Meikles Hotel. Tea is still served in its big lobby every afternoon. The crowd that gathers for tea at Meikles these days includes many blacks, who in the old days were seen at the Meikles only if they were waiters or porters. But the custom of formal tea is dying out, and most people skip it these days and go home after work or school for dinner.

People can buy almost anything they wish to prepare for dinner. A wide variety is available in cities like Harare and Bulawayo. Beef, veal, lamb, and fish can be bought. Fresh vegetables can be found almost anywhere, in rich abundance. City-dwelling Zimbabweans don't eat much differently than Americans do, although there are special touches.

Black Zimbabweans like meat stew as an evening meal, spiced hot enough to make a person's ears feel as if they were on fire. Sometimes the dish is meat and grain, without a broth. Everyone eats from a large common bowl, reaching in with the hands. Broth or not, silverware or not, black Zimbabwean cooking has one consistent feature: it is spicy, hot and spicy.

Africans love beer, and most villages make their own from their own recipe. When villagers move to the city, they take the recipe with them. One homemade beer, made from corn, is called *chibuku*.

In the black townships of Harare and Bulawayo, people cook these meals outside over wood fires whenever they can. At the end of the day, when the evening meals are on the fire, a cloud of smoke sometimes hangs in the air over the townships. It is thick and it bites the eyes. A visitor might say how terrible it is that those people should have to put up with that smoke. But that smoke isn't always a bad thing. For many Africans there is something traditional and sentimental about cooking over wood fires. Perhaps it reminds them of their childhood villages. Perhaps it is something rooted in African legend and lore that non-Africans are just beginning to learn about. In any case, many Africans love it and insist on it. For instance, often in southern Africa a house servant will make sure he or she can have a wood fire before agreeing to take a job in a fancier neighborhood!

Fun in the City

There are things to do everywhere, for both Zimbabweans and travelers. The good weather means that a lot of fun can be had outdoors. Sports are very popular. Soccer draws big crowds, black and white, to the major stadiums, and less important games on lesser playing fields draw onlookers, too. Rugby is also big, mainly among whites. When a big soccer or rugby sports match is televised from England, a lot of Zimbabweans drop everything else and refuse to budge from their television sets.

There are also first-rate golf courses in and near the

cities. Zimbabwe had produced some world-champion golfers, and golfing's a popular pastime. Lawn bowling, another English game imported here, is played by many older whites on well-kept grass courts. In it, two teams roll balls (called bowls), toward a target ball, not pins as in American bowling.

Fishing is something many Zimbabweans love. They fish in rivers and in the lakes that are formed behind dams. These fishing grounds are not far from the cities, and many people take advantage of them.

There are wild game parks, somewhat like zoos, on the edges of both Harare and Bulawayo. People from the cities like to drive through them in the evenings, when the animals are on the move.

Young people hang around the record shops or ice cream parlors. There is a putt-putt golf course in Harare and a drive-in movie. (American films are the favorites, particularly of the young people, as are British films.)

In the villages where many city people were born, it was the custom for men and women to gather in some common place to have a drink and talk. There are beer halls in the city townships where many people go in the evenings. There they see their friends, visit, and talk, as at the gatherings in their villages. The beer halls are operated by the township governors, and the profits are spent on public projects in the same townships.

On weekends, many city dwellers like to get into the

country. Even though small roads are sometimes just a track in the grass, Zimbabwe has a fine system of highways. Its main roads compare well with America's. It is not a long drive in any direction to several national parks or to shrines such as the Matopos Hills. Many places have cabins that can be rented for overnight stays. The outstanding "tourist" places and natural wonders are just as popular with Zimbabweans as they are with visitors; Zimbabweans make repeated visits to places like Victoria Falls and Great Zimbabwe.

Zimbabwe also has a good system of trains for passengers as well as freight. People often take the train on longer trips. Many blacks travel back to their villages on the weekends, particularly those whose families have remained behind while they work in the city. Sometimes, when there is a long weekend, the travelers outward bound from Harare and Bulawayo look like a migration instead of just weekend travelers.

But overnight trips are for weekends or holidays. Perhaps the most popular recreation of all, on workday evenings, is the television set, which seems to be everywhere. Often cultural programs are broadcast in the Shona or Ndebele languages. They feature a lot of dancing and singing, with the actors in traditional dress. The government sometimes broadcasts its own programs, usually some official explaining a public program.

Zimbabweans are frequent visitors to "tourist" spots in the country, like these two people, who have brought an umbrella to keep off the spray from Victoria Falls.

What most Zimbabweans, white and black, wait
for are the American programs. Tom Selleck, of *Mag-
num, P.I.,* is very, very popular with Zimbabweans and
with people all over Africa. Zimbabweans are also fasci-
nated with *The Jeffersons* because they are blacks who
have prospered.

But by 11 p.m., in a country that believes in getting
up early in the morning, the beer halls are closed and
most of the television sets have been shut off. Even in
the modern cities, Africa demands long days of hard
work from its people. For most of them, the rule is early
to bed.

7. *The Bush Country*

Life in Zimbabwe's countryside is different. It is hard, but rewarding and exciting. The broad plains and the endless skies remind people that here nature reigns. In the bush, the great winds blow unchecked, and sometimes so much dust whirls up that the sky turns brown. The rains, when they come, thunder down with such force that people and huts can be swept away by the water. Animals roam, just as wild as ever.

Whether they live in villages with mud huts or on big farms in modern homes, Zimbabweans who make their homes in the countryside are never out of touch with natural forces. Every day, as they go about their business, they may suddenly find themselves absolutely alone for a moment amid the vastness that is Africa. It is like being alone in the world, and that is a special feeling. The air is so clean and fresh in the bush that it seems as if it has been flavored with something. The water in the creeks and rivers, when there has been rain, is pure and unpolluted.

But this aloneness often means lots of hard work. The people of the bush, because their villages and farms are often a long way from the cities, learn to do many things for themselves. Self-reliance is a way of life for

most of them. Many villagers still grow or hunt all their own food, and some make their own clothes. A farm man or woman may have to act as doctor for the family and the people living nearby.

In the countryside, Zimbabweans live in villages, on farms, and in small towns. The towns are almost always located where they are because of some industrial activity, like a mine. For instance, Umtali, the main city in the eastern part of Zimbabwe, is the site of an oil refinery. A city like Umtali has stores, schools, a small hospital, some local government offices, and perhaps an army camp or communications office. But mainly, life in Zimbabwe's bush means life in the villages or life on one of the big farms.

Village Living

Homes in the villages are huts. Many still have walls of mud and roofs of bush grass. Some are made of more modern materials such as cement block and even brick, but even these have thatched roofs in the old style. The huts are small when compared to modern homes. Most have just one room, for sleeping. Cooking and washing are done outside.

Usually the residents of a village are all members of the same clan, or family. Their huts are grouped together. This is a practical arrangement which has been

Smaller towns that spring up around mines and oil sites have simple houses, schools, and stores compared to larger cities, as this picture from the 1950s shows.

handed down from earlier days when villagers had to see to their own protection. Everybody would sleep close by everyone else, in case of an attack during the night or an invasion of wild animals. Even though both are more rare now, the huts are still close together.

Modern government reaches farther and farther into the bush all the time. Still, another old custom is followed in the villages—each has a headman, a leader, to whom the rest look for guidance and judgment. The headman is almost always an older man. Now and then you hear of a village that has a headwoman, but not very often.

More and more village children go to school all the time. Motor vehicles are no longer uncommon. Most villagers have at least had a glimpse of television on their trips to the towns. Yet, despite all those modern things, there are still many villages where people live almost exactly the way their ancestors did, according to the old ways of Africa.

These people have no clocks. Day starts for them when the sun rises, and it ends when the sun sets. Electric lights lengthen the day in the cities and towns and on the big farms, but village people live by nature's light, not something artificial.

Their homes are made of nature's materials: twigs, thick leaves, and mud. They know, because their mothers and grandmothers taught them, how to spin cloth

Even if they are constructed of modern materials, like this store, buildings in the bush often have a thatched roof made from dried plants.

from the fibers of plants. They plant gardens with corn and vegetables, and when they want meat they hunt the antelope and other deer-family species. They can make fishing nets from vines, or spear fish with sticks that were cut from trees and sharpened on rocks.

When people in more modern places want to build a pen for cattle, they buy barbed wire and build a fence. African villagers find barbed wire growing in the bush. They go out and locate some thornbush, a tall bush that resembles a lilac bush. On its long, thin stalks grow terrible thorns, perhaps two inches long. The villagers cut many stalks, carry them back to the village, and tie them together upright like a fence. The thorns stay sharp forever, and no goat or cow tries twice to push through them.

A thornbush fence does not clash with its surroundings the way a barbed wire fence does, because a thornbush fence is part of the surroundings. It looks perfectly natural because it is. But using thornbush for a fence makes another point, too. People who choose to live in the African bush must make use of everything they can, everything nature gives them.

It is rare to see litter in the bush. Everything must be used; something that might, just might, have another use is saved, not thrown away. Other people might look on a rusted metal pot with a hole in it as useless, but a Zimbabwean villager would take it. He or she would break it up and use the sharp pieces as knives.

Food scraps—the rinds of a melon, the bones of an animal—are simply thrown on the ground at some distance away from the village, but this is not littering. By morning the scraps are gone. Nature's scavengers—the hyenas, jackals, or insects—have seen to them.

African villages are often cleaner than the cities where people live in much more modern ways. It is not uncommon to find a village where the ground around the huts has been finely raked. These villages have the same neat appearance as a well-vacuumed living room.

New Ways and Old Traditions

There is a timeless sameness to the day in many remote villages in Zimbabwe. The men hunt and fish. The women tend the gardens and grind corn into flour. The young boys tend the cattle and the cows. Infants go everywhere their mothers go, strapped to their mothers' backs. Young girls help their mothers and at the same time watch over the toddlers. In the villages, everyone helps.

These are days almost exactly like the days their ancestors lived. Yet, changes come. The first white settlers taught African men to work for money, and at one time required it. Today there are villages where all the men board buses or trucks in the morning for a ride to the farm or the mine where they work for wages. Hunting and fishing are left for evenings or the weekends.

Some men work many, many miles from their villages and see their families only on weekends or on holidays. These villages are no longer the same as villages were in the days of the ancestors. Some men leave Zimbabwe entirely and travel to places like South Africa for jobs.

That breaks down the old way of village living, and

so does schooling. More and more children of the villages are required to go to school today than ever before. In school they learn of the big cities of Zimbabwe and of the much bigger world beyond Zimbabwe. Some choose not to return to village life; they want to see more modern things.

Those who do return to the villages bring new ideas with them, and that sometimes causes conflict. An example is the matter of whether a young girl will marry someone she chooses or someone her father chooses.

Women have always held an honored place in traditional African life, as bearers of children and as important business people. It is women, not men, who grow the gardens and who often sell what they grow in the markets. The top-ranking business people in traditional African communities are the market women. Often their family's fortune rests entirely on them, and they are respected because of this.

Yet it is also an African tradition that the father chooses a husband for his daughters. Under old custom, followed as rigidly as any written law in many villages, a daughter is the property of her father until she is married. Upon marriage, she becomes the property of her husband and a member of his family, clan, and tribe.

The government of Robert Mugabe has passed new laws that begin to give young African women more say over their own lives. The laws say that each is recog-

Young children are often looked after by older brothers and sisters.

nized as a person all by herself and has a right to some free choice about her destiny. Even more changes are planned as Zimbabwe and all its people modernize. But it is likely that the old ways will always live in some corners of Zimbabwe. The bush is so big it cannot all be modernized at once. Down this trail or over that hill, there will probably be some place that looks exactly as it always has, where people live in the old ways.

The Large Farms

Zimbabwe's big farms were built by the whites. Before whites arrived, a village or a clan grew only what it needed for itself. The whites introduced cash farming, where they grew great amounts of grain or tobacco to be sold for money in the cities and throughout Africa and Europe. The whites took the best land and a lot of it. Some white farms are measured in square miles, not in acres. The whites farmed so well that Rhodesia became known as "the breadbasket of Africa."

Because of their size and their locations, many of these farms are as remote as the villages are. Sometimes a farmer who has work to do on the far end of his spread will have to be gone several days, even though he never leaves his own property. While he is gone, his family may have to oversee the rest of his farm.

In many cases, a big white farm is a community all

Some farms in Zimbabwe stretch for miles. A farmhouse can just be seen in the left of the photo.

by itself. There is the farmer and his family, the farm manager with his or her family, and the black workers who live on the farm, often with their families. The food that has to be bought is purchased in large quantities to avoid too-frequent trips to town. Farm supplies and replacement tools also have to be kept on hand.

Everyone works, just as in the villages. Few Zimbabwean farmers can afford the luxury of watching others work. Most spend long days in the field with the workers, even though they may be quite well-to-do. Farm women often set up schools for the young children, both black and white, when the real schools are too far away to send youngsters. The women also have to be doctor and nurse, because the real doctor and the hospital may be far away.

The children of the farmer, from their early teen years, usually have responsibilities of their own. It might be tending the family garden, helping with the ploughing, or tending the riding horses. Both the sons and daughters raised on the big farms learn early to drive a tractor and to hoe a garden patch.

Shortwave radios put the big farms in touch with each other, and connect them with the police and the military. The closest neighboring farm is often a good drive away. Usually a farm family will travel by car or truck when they go visiting, although sometimes they will ride their horses. A child's closest friend might be miles and miles away. Trips on the highways to the cities of Harare and Bulawayo are overnight trips for many farm families.

On the large farms there is usually a lot of hired help, household help as well as farm workers, and that makes life easier and allows some time for fun. Since farm families have to arrange their recreation themselves—movie theaters are far away—a lot of the farms have swimming pools, and a lot of farm children have ponies. Most of the farms have television.

The countryside is big, and sometimes might seem pretty empty. But big, empty spaces also give some people a feeling of freedom, a feeling that they are totally in charge of their own affairs. Some of the white farmers, like their ancestors, would not trade this feeling of freedom for all the bright lights in the cities.

Since independence, a major effort has been made by the government to train more blacks to farm on a big scale. Food is essential to Africa and to Zimbabwe. Without it, as Ethiopia taught us in the 1980s, the people suffer terribly and die by the hundreds. The ability to grow food has always been a strong point of Rhodesia and Zimbabwe, and the government does not want this to change.

Some white farmers left after the civil war, choosing not to live under black rule. Their farms have been taken over by the government, which broke them up

Farmhands and their families relax at homes on a large farm after a day's work.

into smaller farms for black farmers being trained in modern methods.

Country Delights

For fun, both black villagers and white farm families turn to the countryside itself. White children learn to hunt and fish and camp at an early age. They all ride horses early. The outdoors is their life. They may be far away from other children on their farms and their villages, but all children know about sports. They all know what to do with a soccer ball. They also know how to make one if no one has one: stuff a sack tightly with rags or leaves, wrap twine or vine snugly around it, and kick away.

Find a way. That's the rule in the villages and on the farms. Make what you don't have. And make even chores more fun. Can work be fun? It may not be fun to follow a herd of goats or cows around all afternoon, as many a village boy must do. But it's fun to shoo a cow into a river, then grab its tail and be pulled across.

There are other excitements in bush life. Everyone who lives in Zimbabwe's countryside has a tale to tell about wild animals.

For instance, there's the story about the farm woman who missed her card game because of the elephants. The woman lived near Beitbridge, the main crossing over the Limpopo River between Zimbabwe and South Africa. She got into her Morris automobile (a British car that is so tiny it looks like a toy) and she drove off in a hurry toward another farm to play bridge.

She was late already when she rounded a curve and found a herd of elephants blocking the road. The woman stopped her car and waited. And waited. She looked at her watch and she waited some more. But the elephants didn't move.

Finally she blew the car's horn. That was a mistake. The elephants now took notice of the noisy little car, and all of them stared at it. Then the bull elephant, leader of the herd, walked slowly over to the car, worked his trunk under it, and rolled it off the road and into the deep bush grass, leaving it upside down. Then the bull walked back to the herd and the elephants resumed whatever they had been doing when the woman drove up.

It was hours later (and the elephants were long gone) when another driver came along and noticed the woman's car on its roof in the grass. He freed her and found that she was unhurt. But she was speechless. It was hours before she could explain to anyone what had happened.

Animal excitements aren't always that personal, but they do exist in most corners of Zimbabwe. You may look at a meadow and see nothing but bush grass. Then, suddenly, dozens and dozens of impala, who were standing there all along, will jump into the air at once in some wild African dance. It is ballet that takes your breath away.

The End of the Day

Work ends in the bush with sundown, and it is a special time. Darkness begins to fall over the great plains, and people head for home, the villagers to their huts and the farmers to the farm house. The stars are coming; there are so many they look like salt sprinkled on the sky. It is in some ways a spiritual moment, day's end, a reminder of the natural order of things.

Meals are on the fire. In the village it will be mealies, made either as a corn flour pudding or bread. Corn is the food of life all over the continent. Hardly any traditional African meal is served without mealies. In the villages, the women grind kernels of corn between two rocks to make this dish.

There might be melon with the mealies, or vegetables, or wild berries, and often there is meat from some wild animal. On special occasions, one of the village goats will be roasted. Tea is served in gourds at village meals, and there is the village beer. Wood smoke from the open fires is the sign to villagers that they are about to eat.

At the white farmhouse, supper might be steak on the grill or a roast in the oven. Potatoes, vegetables from the house garden, and dessert brought from the city might accompany the meal. Trifle, the wonderful English dessert pudding, is popular with white Zimbabweans (and with just about everyone else who has tasted it).

It is interesting that white farmers and black villagers celebrate sundown in quite the same way. Traditionally, on the white farms everyone gathers on the porch

Sundown is a special time in the bush.

of the main house to watch the sun go down and to talk over the day. Whites call these gatherings Sundowners. In the villages, at the same moment, families will be gathering around the common fire. The men rest and talk, the boys and girls run and laugh, and the mothers play with the babies.

It is as if everyone who lives in the bush is drawn to be with others at this moment, when the sun goes down and another day ends. There is something magical and wonderful about it.

African Cooking

Following are two recipes, one dinner dish that villagers might prepare and one dessert recipe that whites brought from England to Zimbabwe. Both have been changed so that they can be made in American kitchens.

Green Mealie Pudding

1 tablespoon butter, softened
2 tablespoons butter, melted, then cooled
3 cups freshly cut corn kernels (from about six ears
   of corn) *or* 3 cups frozen corn kernels, defrosted
2 tablespoons flour
2 tablespoons sugar
1 teaspoon salt
2 teaspoons baking powder
pastry brush
an 8" x 4" x 2" loaf pan
blender
aluminum foil
extra baking pan (9" x 9" or 13"x 9")

1. Preheat the oven to 375 degrees. Using the pastry brush, spread the tablespoon of softened butter on the bottom and sides of the pan.

2. Put the corn and the eggs in the blender container and blend ten seconds at high speed. Stop, scrape down the mixture, then blend for another ten seconds. (The mixture should still contain some small pieces of corn.) Add the melted butter, flour, sugar, salt, and baking powder. Blend again for a few seconds, until ingredients are mixed.

3. Put the mixture in the loaf pan. Cover the pan with a doubled piece of foil, pinching the foil all around the pan. Set the loaf pan into the larger baking dish, and pour boiling water into the larger pan until it is halfway up the loaf pan's sides.

4. Bake the pudding for 1 hour, or until a knife in its center comes out clean. Remove the loaf pan, uncover it, and let it sit out for five to ten minutes. Run a knife along the edges to loosen the pudding. Invert a serving plate over the loaf pan and then flip the pudding onto the plate. Tap the bottom of the pan if the pudding sticks.

Mealie pudding can be served hot or at room temperature. Cut into half-inch slices.

Trifle

6 egg yolks, lightly beaten
1/3 cup sugar
3 cups milk, heated until almost boiling
1 teaspoon vanilla
sponge cake (2 layers) or ladyfingers (about 12)
apricot, strawberry, or raspberry jam
1/2 cup dry sherry or orange juice
1 cup heavy whipping cream
1/3 cup slivered almonds
candied cherries
large saucepan
wire whisk or electric mixer

1. Put the egg yolks, sugar, and hot milk in the saucepan. Beat with the mixer or whisk to mix well. Heat mixture over medium heat, stirring often, until it thickens. Remove from heat, stir in vanilla, and set aside to cool.

2. Place sponge cake layer, or about six ladyfingers, in the bottom of the glass bowl. Spread a thin layer of jam over the cake, then sprinkle on the sherry or orange juice. Repeat with a second layer of cake, jam, and sherry or juice. Set aside to let the liquid soak into the cake.

3. Whip the heavy cream with the whisk or mixer
    until soft peaks form. Pour the completely-
    cooled pudding over the cake in the bowl. Top
    with whipped cream and decorate with nuts
    and cherries.

8. An African Education

Those of us born in America or in Canada would feel quite at home in school in Zimbabwe, because most of the teaching is done in English, the country's official language. But language study doesn't stop with just English. Each of us would have to take courses in Zimbabwe's main native languages, the Shona and Ndebele languages. There is no skipping these classes. They are required by the government. Everyone must learn everyone else's languages, at least a little bit.

The reason for this is found in a belief held by the government of Prime Minister Mugabe when the new nation came into being in 1980. If Zimbabwe is to succeed, they said, everyone must work together, white, Shona, or Ndebele. Conflicts between people of different colors or groups will probably always exist. But if different people can talk with each other and get to know each other, perhaps their differences will not cause trouble. So a rule was made that each child must learn all of the languages of the country. It is meant to break down barriers between them.

Other school policies also reflect Zimbabwe's newness and the challenges it faces. Every child must take courses in agriculture. If Africa does not have enough to eat, its people suffer and its governments are weakened. This is true even in a rich country like Zimbabwe. Food comes first, and everyone must be trained to know it and to help.

In schools great importance is also placed on what Zimbabwe calls "education for production." Zimbabwe inherited a modern economy when black rule replaced white rule, and a modern economy needs many workers in trades, such as carpenters, plumbers, electricians, railroad engineers, highway builders, and mine supervisors. Not everyone can have an office job. Skilled workers are needed in large numbers if the Zimbabwean economy is to go forward. Therefore, "education for production" teaches Zimbabwean students that blue-collar jobs are important to the country and should make people just as proud as any other sort of job.

Finally, Africa's wish to take its rightful place in the modern world is reflected in Zimbabwe's choice of English as its official language and the main language of the schools. It would have been easy (and perhaps natural and understandable) for Zimbabwe to ban English when white rule was finally overthrown. The new government could have chosen an African tongue as the official language. But English is more and more the main language of international affairs and international trade. English prepares Zimbabweans to be comfortable in those areas.

Children must study three languages while they are in school.

Education for Modern Times

Most Africans thirst for education. Parents will work extra long hours to see that their children can go to school. The children work hard, too. It is not unusual to see school children sitting on the city curbs at night, studying by the light of the streetlights because there are no electric lights in their homes.

The importance of education was shown right from the beginning of the new government in 1980. Two major goals were announced: some sort of health care for all, and education for all.

Schooling for every single child is the plan in Zimbabwe, but it has not yet come about. It is difficult for the government to get every child into school. There are still many people living in the remote countryside of Zimbabwe. There, their lives follow the old, old pattern of their ancestors. They raise cattle, fish the rivers, and hoe gardens. They speak the dialect of their people, whether the world understands it or not. Although all of them have seen motor vehicles on the roads and airplanes in the sky, they have little personal contact with the modern world, and schooling as we think of it means little to them.

Their boys are trained to tend the goats and the cattle and to hunt and fish, just as their fathers and grandfathers were trained. Why, they wonder, do they need English or math? Their girls are trained to tend the gardens and go to market and care for babies. Why, they ask, do they need to study science from a book, or literature? A boy or girl of ten already has responsibilities in the family, important responsibilities, and they do not have time to sit in a schoolroom.

Getting these boys and girls into school, and keeping them there, means persuading their elders that a new day has dawned for everyone in Zimbabwe. The government argues that their children will inherit a modern nation and will need new and modern skills. It does not always work. Many people cling to their old ways and keep their children out of school.

Also, there are the nomads, who move from place to place. How does Zimbabwe (and the rest of Africa) bring education to its people who migrate, when they are here today and somewhere else in a few months?

Lack of money has also slowed Zimbabwe's progress toward education for all. It costs a great deal of money to build new schools everywhere at once and to train and hire enough teachers. In 1981 and 1982, prices for the products of Zimbabwe's mines and farms fell, and there were hard times for many as a result. That meant less money for the government to use for schools and other good purposes.

Yet much progress has been made. The government reports many more children attending at least primary school than in the days of white rule.

There are so many children enrolled in some areas that are short of school buildings that the seats in the classrooms never cool off. One set of elementary children will report for school early in the morning. When they leave, another set moves in. Later the desks may be

For years, schools in Zimbabwe were segregated, and black children had fewer opportunities for schooling than whites. Farm schools such as this one, started in the 1960s, were sometimes the only schools for miles around.

used by high school students. Some school buildings are full from first light in the morning until dark.

During white rule, formal schools were segregated. There were separate schools for blacks and whites. One of the rare exceptions to this was the farm schools. Some farms were so far from the schools of the cities that the young children would have to stay at school overnight. Rather than do that, some farm families started their own schools at home, the best-educated farm woman in the area serving as teacher. Some of these farm schools included not only the white children of the farmers but the black children of the farm hands. Today, under the new government, all schools are integrated. Black and white study together.

The School Years

Primary education is free. The government supports it, supplies the building, and pays the teachers. But high school, for many students, is not free. Parents are expected to pay something in tuition if they are at all able to do so.

Elementary education lasts nine years. Those who go beyond elementary school can go to two different kinds of high schools. There are college preparatory high schools for the best students. College prep high school lasts six years, not four years as in the United States. Those Zimbabwean children who do not go to college prep schools are put in vocational high schools, where they are taught the skills that equip them for jobs in a modern economy. Vocational high school lasts four years.

Many children go no farther than elementary school. The dropout rate is much too high for the government's liking. In 1982, according to one count, almost two million children were enrolled in elementary

Students compete at every level for the best grades in order to win scholarships and places at other schools.

schools, but only 225,000 were in high schools. More schools, more teachers, and more persuasion are needed.

At every level of school, there is intense competition. Students try to get the best grades in class. When elementary school is finished, they wonder, who will be the lucky ones to win spots in the college preparatory high school? When high school is finished, who will get the scholarships to college? Who will do so well in

college that he or she will be sent to England for more
training, or to America? Education, to many African
families, is the key to everything that is good, everything
that will bring more pride to Africa and a better life to
its people. It is a very serious thing.

Studies

What are Zimbabwean children taught in school,
besides each other's languages, agriculture, and education for production? The same things children study in
school all over the world: science, mathematics, history,
geography, spelling, reading, and literature. And as they
do in many countries, the children learn things that will
first help them understand Zimbabwe, then Africa, and
then other parts of the world.

Does it strike you as unfair to expect black African
children to study subjects like science and literature in
English, someone else's language, rather than in their
own language? The students might smile at that and tell
you not to worry for them. Africans in general have an
amazing talent for languages. They are not nervous
about tackling a foreign language; instead, many of
them will learn it rapidly. There are schools in Africa
where seventh- and eighth-graders study two and three
different languages, all in the same semester!

Why are Africans so good at languages? Some

scholars say it is because the spoken word is so important to them. Little of ancient African history was ever
written down. Instead, it was passed from one generation to another by word of mouth, in songs or in stories.
This meant that everyone had to listen well, if the stories
were to survive. Good ears were a must.

Africans, of all ages, are great listeners. Words are
very important to them. When they greet a visitor or bid
one farewell, they often make a little speech, and they
choose the words with great care. When someone talks
in another language, they listen with the same great
care. Their ears seem to adjust to the new sounds of a
different language, and in a short time they seem comfortable with it and begin to use it as one of theirs.

One of the delights of traveling to Africa is to find
yourself alone with Africans and to use a word they
have not heard before. They jump on it as if you had
given them a present. They repeat it, sounding it out.
They ask to hear it again. They talk about it among
themselves, in their own languages, trying to figure it
out. When they do, they are absolutely thrilled. Then it
is their word, too. African curiosity and love of language have made it so.

9. Fame Abroad

Very few Zimbabweans are known to the wider world, and the reasons are not difficult to guess. Africa lay unknown for all the centuries before whites came. The whites who settled in Zimbabwe in the last century had so much to do just making homes and staying alive that very few of them had time for the sort of activities that bring worldwide fame. Then came the long war for independence, when everything took a back seat to the fighting.

So it should not come as too much of a surprise that the best-known Zimbabwean is still the first of the white Rhodesians, Cecil John Rhodes. A few others have gained international success as well. One is Doris Lessing, the novelist, who grew up in Rhodesia and now lives in England. Another is the professional golfer Denis Watson, who won a great deal of money in 1984 on the American golf tour.

But after them, the Zimbabweans we know best are those who led the opposing sides in the civil war: Ian Smith, the last white prime minister, Robert Mugabe, and Joshua Nkomo.

The Zimbabwe Embassy in Washington estimates that there were no more then 200 to 300 Zimbabweans in America in the 1980s, most of them students. More Zimbabweans can be found in England, which is closer to Africa and to which the country has had ties since the first whites arrived. Some of these who are students there go to England courtesy of Cecil Rhodes.

Dreams Without Limits

Rhodes, the diamond billionaire who first led white settlers to what is now Zimbabwe, was a fascinating fellow. When he was a poor young student in England, he wrote a will giving away his fortune to causes he thought good ones. He was so sure that he would make a great fortune that he wrote the will first! But when Rhodes made the fortune, it was great indeed.

He was a man of dreams that had no limits. Many people thought his dream of English colonies stretching from the bottom of Africa to the top was impossible, but he did not. He thought nothing impossible for good Christians who were willing to work hard. He dreamed of an English railroad through Africa, linking South Africa and Egypt. And he had another dream. When he was finished with Africa, he planned to bring America back into the English family of colonies. (Of course, the United States declared its independence from England in 1776 and made it stick.) Rhodes' death ended his dreams. But he did manage to change the world, in a way.

Cecil Rhodes, who led the first white settlers into Zimbabwe.

Many people regard Rhodes as a racist, because he believed that white Christians were chosen to educate and civilize all the other people of the world. In his final will he left three million English pounds, an enormous amount of money in 1902, as a fund for the famous Rhodes Scholarships. Rhodes intended for the brightest young men from the British colonies, the United States, and Germany—those likely to be the next leaders of the Western world—to be educated at Oxford University in England from his fortune.

Historians who have studied Rhodes' life, his writings, and his statements feel he never fully gave up his belief that whites were superior. But his will said nothing about giving his scholarships to white men only, and many nonwhites have gone to study in England on them. So have women. Rhodes' will spoke of young "men," but today the word "men" is taken to mean that all human beings can be granted Rhodes Scholarships. Zimbabwe can send three scholars every other year to Oxford.

Time swept past Rhodes. His greatest dreams fell short. Zimbabwe no longer bears his name. The great British Empire he believed in so deeply is gone. But his name still lives, and not only because of his scholars. He was a man with grand visions, however we might disagree with what he foresaw, and for many years in Africa hardly anyone stood taller.

African Novelist

Doris Lessing, the author, was disturbed by the way whites in Rhodesia treated blacks during the years when whites ran everything. White herself, she became a sharp critic of Rhodesia.

Ms. Lessing was born in Persia (now Iran) seventeen years after Rhodes' death. Her father was a British army officer, and in the days of the great British Empire army officers and their families could be sent almost anywhere. Ms. Lessings' family came to Rhodesia in 1924, when she was just about five, and in Africa she grew up. She attended elementary school at a Catholic convent and secondary school at Girls' High School, both in Salisbury (Harare). She left school when she was fourteen, convinced at that time that she had no talent for anything. But today she is regarded as one of the best novelists of the post-World War II years.

She moved to England in 1949, partly to get away from what she regarded as the racialism of her homeland. (Americans say racism; the English say racialism.)

Her first novel, which is set in Rhodesia, is called *The Grass Is Singing*. It was published in 1950. In it, a woman who lives on an isolated farm is killed by her black houseboy, whom she treated cruelly. After that, Ms. Lessing wrote five books in a series called "Children of Violence," which also dealt with blacks and whites in Rhodesian society. In 1964, she published *African Stories*.

Ms. Lessing's fame is due in great measure to her other books, which are not about Africa but about men and women and their places in the world. Yet Africa touched her deeply and marked her. Africa, she said in an interview, "is not a place to visit unless one chooses to be an exile ever afterwards . . . . Africa gives you the knowledge that man is a small creature. . . ."

Ms. Lessing has said that World War II awakened her to the possibility that racism could be overturned. The war brought many people from different lands to Africa and to Rhodesia. For the first time, she said, she met people who not only despised racism but were willing to do something about it. Her writings reflected her own distaste for white rule and, when the bitterness in Rhodesia turned to war, she was stopped from returning to her homeland and from visiting neighboring South Africa.

Sports Players from Zimbabwe

Sports have always been important in Africa and in the British Empire. Soccer spread around the world in the trunks of England's empire-builders, because so little equipment was needed. All you really needed was the ball. In Rhodesia, soccer or rugby (English football) was the top sport, depending on which you preferred.

But racial politics kept Rhodesia out of great tournaments like soccer's World Cup, where its stars might have become famous. Rhodesia wanted to enter competition for the World Cup in 1968, but the newly-independent black nations of Africa refused to play against them. When Rhodesia tried to join the African

Football Confederation in the early 1970s, the result was the same. The other soccer-playing African countries didn't believe Rhodesia's promise to have a team that included blacks, and Rhodesia was not allowed in.

Therefore, if Rhodesia had a soccer player worthy of world recognition during the years of white rule, there was no big "stage" on which he could show his stuff. Since independence, Zimbabwe has been slowly building a new national sports program, but it is not yet well known.

Golf is another sport the British carried with them around the world. There are wonderful golf courses on which to play in all the old British colonies in Africa, thanks to those colonists. Perhaps because golf is an individual's sport, rather than a team sport, a couple of players from Zimbabwe have been able to get to places where the world might notice them.

Denis Watson is one of them. He was born in Harare and learned golf there. Then he went to South Africa, where there are more players and better competition. Finally he came to the United States. In 1984 he won the World Series of Golf and two other tournaments. Another golfer who played a great deal in Zimbabwe is Nick Price. He was born in South Africa, but he moved to Zimbabwe to serve as caddy for a brother who was a golf professional there. Price also has won the World Series of Golf.

Politicans and the Future

Authors and golfers, however, take second place in many eyes to the black and white politicans of Zimbabwe, since it is the country's politics and racial policies which have gotten so much attention.

It is Robert Mugabe and Joshua Nkomo whose names dominate the news wires that carry the happenings of Zimbabwe to the world at large today. During the war the name of Ian Smith, the prime minister, symbolized white refusal to give in to change.

Smith is one of Zimbabwe's white farmers. He continued in politics, even after he stopped being prime minister. He became one of the white senators under Zimbabwe's new constitution. Smith fought in World WII, and he required a lot of surgery to rebuild his face after his fighter plane crashed. Like many of Rhodesia's whites, he could have left the country after the war; but he regarded Africa as his home, and he stayed.

But now the world looks to Zimbabwe's black leaders. Each of them, Nkomo and Mugabe, shared the same dream for their country—rule by the black majority—but each had his own style, and they clashed frequently. Nkomo always seemed more open to compromise with the white settlers. Nkomo, older than Mugabe, was a groundbreaker in some ways; he had gotten a degree in social work, one of the few Rhodesian blacks of the time to get a college education.

Mugabe always talked tougher. Mugabe went to college at the University of Fort Hare in South Africa, where many leaders of the African independence movements had been trained. He also lived for some years in Ghana, where he came under the influence of fiery Kwame Nkrumah, a leader in the African independence movement.

Both Nkomo and Mugabe suffered at the hands of the white regime in Rhodesia. In the 1960s, when black demands for political freedom were growing in strength, each was arrested a number of times. Both were made to live under house arrest in remote government camps for a full ten years, from the early 1960s into the 1970s. But each continued the struggle in confinement, by teaching other prisoners or by writing. Later, Nkomo and Mugabe had to leave Rhodesia. Each directed guerilla armies from exile in neighboring countries. Both leaders traveled to the United Nations in New York at different times to tell the world how Africans in Zimbabwe were not free in their own land. Each won much support there.

The world watches these two closely today, and with some nervousness. Many people who know Africa feel that whether Zimbabwe continues to thrive and to fulfill its promise depends heavily on whether these two men can get along.

Prime Minister Robert Mugabe and Sally Mugabe celebrated three years of independence in 1983. The world wonders what Zimbabwe's future holds.

Since independence they have quarrelled as much as they have worked together. In 1983, Nkomo slipped across a border at night and fled to England, charging that Mugabe's troops were searching for him to kill him. Mugabe has blamed unrest in the south of Zimbabwe on Nkomo's followers. Some people say the quarrels between the two leaders have to do with the old differences. The Shona and Ndebele always fought, they say. Others suggest that the differences are personal, that both Nkomo and Mugabe want to be on top.

Nkomo returned from exile in 1984 and became a candidate against Mugabe in the national elections scheduled for early 1985. But violence broke out during the campaigning, with a number of politicians and their supporters murdered. The elections were postponed, at least for a number of months.

In its own way, the unrest is as dangerous to Zimbabwe and its dreams as the drought of the early 1980s was. The world watches to see if Zimbabwe can avoid the fate of other free African nations, where today blacks treat other blacks in much the same way that some colonial governments treated them.

Zimbabwe and the United States

Americans played important roles in Zimbabwe in both the earliest days of white exploration and in the struggle that led to the new government. Adam Renders, the explorer and trader who first stumbled on the ruins of Great Zimbabwe, was an American. He also was something of a man of mystery. Little is known of him that we can be sure of, except that his home base was in the Transvaal, the northern part of South Africa.

He frequently explored north of the Limpopo River. Renders' discovery of Great Zimbabwe sent the first wave of fortune seekers to the ruins. They thought they would find gold.

During the years of white rule, America was a customer of Rhodesia. U.S. auto makers bought chromium from the Rhodesian mines, which are some of the richest in the world. America has no significant chromium mines of its own.

Two famous Americans played roles in the black movement for independence. One was Henry Kissinger, secretary of state to presidents Richard M. Nixon and Gerald R. Ford. The other was Andrew Young, who was ambassador to the United Nations under President Jimmy Carter.

Kissinger traveled to Lusaka, Zambia during the Ford presidency to try to work out a settlement between the Zimbabwean guerillas and the white rulers of Rhodesia. He failed, as did others.

President Carter, who made human rights an urgent matter of his foreign policy, supported the trade boycott on Rhodesian minerals and farm goods which had been voted by the United Nations. He also voiced support for political freedom for Rhodesia's blacks. His agent in this was Andrew Young, a black man who had been an assistant to the Reverend Martin Luther King. At the United Nations, Young allied himself and the

While he was United Nations ambassador, Andrew Young (right) met with many black Zimbabwean leaders such as Bishop Abel Muzorewa (left).

United States more than ever before with the forces for black rule in Africa. He was outspoken in his support for the guerillas in Rhodesia, and he made several trips to the scene during the civil war. When the white rulers finally gave in but tried to exclude the guerillas from the new black government, both Young and President Carter objected and sided with the guerillas. Andrew Young became mayor of Atlanta, Georgia, but kept in close touch with the leaders of Zimbabwe and other African countries.

Except for the Africans who were brought to it as slaves, the United States for years had little contact with that continent. America never had colonies in Africa. For many, many years, it was simply a mysterious place, far, far away; Americans needed to know no more than that it was full of strange people and animals. Adventure stories about Africa were popular, but few people ever bothered to get to know Africa beyond that.

That situation changed after World War II and the development of the jet airplane. Today, leaving Kennedy Airport in New York, Americans can be in West Africa in little more than six hours. Four or five more hours and the traveler can be in Zimbabwe.

The world has shrunk. Every corner of it is now a neighbor. People have learned that war or human distress in any other part of the world disturbs their peace, too. This has made it necessary for America to get active all over Africa. The United States is especially interested in Zimbabwe, which many people believe can become a model for a free, productive Africa.

America is finally getting to know places like Zimbabwe. When you see it and meet its people, you will wonder why everyone waited so long.

Appendix A

Zimbabwean Embassies and Other Offices in the United States and Canada

Americans and Canadians are not required to get visas before traveling to Zimbabwe. The Republic of Zimbabwe maintains three offices in the U.S. where those interested may request information. They are eager to help Americans and Canadians learn more about Zimbabwe.

U.S. Embassy and Offices

Embassy, Republic of Zimbabwe
2852 McGill Terrace NW
Washington, D.C. 20008
Phone (202) 332-7100

Zimbabwe Mission to the
  United Nations
19 East 47th Street
New York, New York 10017
Phone (212) 980-9511

Zimbabwe Travel Board
35 E. Wacker Drive
Chicago, Illinois 60601
Phone (312) 332-2601

Canadian Office

Zimbabwe High Commission
112 Kemp St., Suite 915
Place de Ville, Tower B
Ottawa, Ontario K1P 5P2
Phone (613) 237-4388

Appendix B

The Languages of the Shona and Ndebele Peoples

Overall in Africa, more than 800 languages are spoken! Usually, people of each black African ethnic group (tribe) have a separate language, although some of the languages are more common than others. These commoner languages are often learned in addition to a person's native tongue, so that that person can communicate with people of different groups.

There are several broad groups, or families, of African languages. The Niger-Kordfanian family of languages, spoken in central and southern Africa, includes hundreds of tongues, including about 300 Bantu languages. Shona and Ndebele both are part of this Bantu language group. Even though they came from the same root language, the two languages developed very differently, as the phrases below show.

English	Shona	Ndebele
Hello.	Kazwayi. (kah·zee·WHY)	Salibonani. (to one person) (sal·ih·BOH·nah·nee) Sakubona. (to two or more) (sak·ooh·BOH·nah)
Goodbye.	Chisarai. (CHIH·sahr·eye)	Salanini kuhle. (sal·ih·NEE·NEE·COO·say)
You are welcome.	Titambereyi. (tit·am·BEHR·eye)	Semukele. (sem·OOH·kee·lee)
These are my children.	Ava zana vangu. (ah·vah zah·nah VAN·goo)	Laba ngabantwana bami. (lah·bah en·gahb·on·TWAH·nah bah·mee)
Will it rain?	Mvura ichanaya here? (em·voo·rah ee·chah·NAH·yah HAIR·ah)	Izulu Lizakuna na? (ee·ZOO·loo liz·ah·KOO·nah nah)
School is fun.	Chikoro chino nakidza. (CHIH·koh·roh CHEE·noh nah·KID·zah)	Isikolo siyatabisa. (issih·KOH·loh see·yah·TAH·BISS·ah)

Glossary

assegai (AH·seh·guy)—a short stabbing African spear

Bantu (BAN·too)—a large group of black African peoples or the languages they speak

Beitbridge (BITE·brij)—a city of southern Zimbabwe

Botswana (bot·SWAN·uh)—country of southern Africa

Bulawayo (boo·lah·WAY·oh)—city in southwest Zimbabwe

bush—the wide open, mainly unpopulated areas of African countries

Chaka (CHOCK·uh)—a Zulu king

Changamire (CHANG·uh·meer)—a nation of Zimbabwe that existed in the 1500s and 1600s

chibuku (chih·BOO·koo)—homemade beer brewed from corn

Dombo (DOM·boh)—a king of the Changamire (later the Rozwi) empire

ethnic (ETH·nik) **group**—related group of people who have race, language, religion, ancestors, and/or culture in common; some African ethnic groups were once referred to as tribes

Ghana (GAH·nah)—nation of central Africa

guerilla (guh·RIL·uh)—a person who fights a war in small battles and sneak attacks rather than in set battles

Harare (huh·RAH·ree)—capital of Zimbabwe, once called Salisbury

Kariba (kuh·REE·buh) **Lake**—lake that formed behind the Kariba Dam on the Zambezi River

Kenya (KEN·yuh)—nation of eastern Africa

kopje (KOP·jee)—hill

Limpopo (lim·POH·poh)—river in southern Zimbabwe

Lobengula (LOH·ben·goo·lah)—Shona king who was ruling when whites came to Zimbabwe

maize (MAYZ)—corn

Matopos (mah·TOH·pohs) **Hills**—an area of oddly shaped rock formations in Zimbabwe

Mashona (mah·SHOW·nah)—another name for the Shona people

Matabele (MAT·uh·bee·lee)—another name for the Ndebele people

McIlwaine (MACK·ill·wayn), **Lake**—reservoir lake in Zimbabwe

mealies (MEE·lees)—a pudding or bread, both made with ground corn

Monomatapa (mon·oh·mah·TAH·pah)—a legendary nation of Zimbabwe which some say built Great Zimbabwe

Mozambique (moh·zam·BEEK)—country of southern Africa

Mugabe (moo·GAH·bee), **Robert**—prime minister of Zimbabwe, starting in 1980

Mutota (moo·TOH·tah)—king who founded the

Monomatapa empire

Muzorewa (moo·zuh·RAY·wah), **Bishop Abel**—black leader in Zimbabwe

Mzilikazi (em·ZILL·ah·kah·zee)—leader of the Ndebele people who led the group north from South Africa to Zimbabwe

Namibia (nah·MIB·ee·ah)—nation of southern Africa

Ndebele (END·uh·bell·ee)—ethnic group making up about 15 percent of Zimbabwe's population

Nkomo (en·KOH·moh), **Joshua**—black leader in Zimbabwe

Nkrumah, Kwame (en·KROO·muh, KWAH·may)—president of Ghana at one time

Rhodes (ROHDZ), **Cecil**—English man who led white settlers into Zimbabwe, and after whom Rhodesia was named

Rhodesia (roh·DEE·zhah)—former name of Zimbabwe

Rozwi (ROZ·wee)—the Shona empire that ruled at the time of the Ndebele invasion into Zimbabwe

Salisbury (SOLS·buh·ree)—former name of Harare

Shona (SHOW·nah)—ethnic group of Zimbabwe which makes up about 80 percent of the population

Sinoia (sin·OY·ah)—city in central Zimbabwe

subsistence (sub·SIS·ten[t]s) **farming**—growing only enough food for one's immediate family or village

Tanzania (tan·zuh·NEE·uh)—nation of eastern Africa

Togwa (TOG·wah)—empire that was absorbed into the Changamire empire

Umtali (oom·TAH·lee)—city in eastern Zimbabwe

Unilateral (you·nee·LAT·uh·rahl) **Declaration of Independence (UDI)**—the act by which the colony of Rhodesia broke away from Great Britain

Whitsunday (hwit·SUN·dee)—Pentecost Sunday

Zambezi (zam·BEE·zee)—river in northern Zimbabwe

Zambia (ZAM·bee·uh)—nation of southern Africa

Zimbabwe (zim·BOB·wee)—formerly the nation of Rhodesia; *zimbabwe* can mean either "stone enclosure" or "structures of stone"

Zulu (ZOO·loo)—ethnic group of South Africa

Selected Bibliography

As of 1985 there were few history books about Zimbabwe. At that time the country was only five years old, and those five years had been filled with problems. A number of books were written during the long war for independence, but those took one side or another, and are slanted in the information they give. There is a reliable book about the early years of Southern Rhodesia that begins with the first explorers:

Gann, L.H. *A History of Southern Rhodesia, to 1934.* New York: Humanities Press, 1969.

Africa under colonial rule is described in:

Cartey, Wilfred and Martin Kilson. *The Africa Reader: Colonial Africa.* New York: Random House, 1970.

Two books that describe Africa's moves toward independence:

Cowan, L. Gray. *The Dilemmas of African Independence.* New York: Walker and Co., 1968.
Ferkiss, Victor G. *Africa's Search for Identity.* Cleveland: World Publishing Company, 1967.

A book for younger readers, with limited information on Zimbabwe:

Taylor, L.B. *South East Africa: Zimbabwe, Zambia, Malawi, Madagascar, Mauritius, and Reunion.* New York: Franklin Watts, 1981.

Index

About the Author

Al Stark is a columnist for *The Detroit News* who in 1983 visited eight different African countries. He gave his impressions of these in a series of newspaper articles. While in Africa, he found Zimbabwe to be most impressive, and chose it as the subject for this, his first book for children.

Mr. Stark feels that children should know more about the nations of Africa and be helped to understand that world and how it is changing. As he says, when people get to know Africa, "They'll wonder why they waited so long."

Al Stark lives in Grosse Pointe Park, Michigan. He has six children.